COLLECTING
TEDDY BEARS
& DOLLS

The Facts At Your Fingertips

COLLECTING
TEDDY BEARS
& DOLLS
The Facts At Your Fingertips

ALISON BECKETT

SPECIAL CONSULTANT:
BUNNY CAMPIONE

Collecting Teddy Bears & Dolls
The Facts At Your Fingertips

First published in Great Britain in 1996 by Miller's, an imprint of
Mitchell Beazley, a division of Octopus Publishing Group Ltd.

This 2002 edition published by Bounty Books, a division of
Octopus Publishing Group Ltd, 2–4 Heron Quays, London E14 4JP

Executive Editor Alison Starling
Executive Art Editor Vivienne Brar
Project Editor Francesca Collin
Text Editors Diane Pengelly, Nance Fyson
Designer Louise Griffiths
Production Jenny May, Dawn Mitchell
Special Photography Tim Ridley, Ian Booth, Jacqui Hurst
Illustrations Simon Miller
Indexer Richard Bird

A CIP catalogue for this book is available from the British Library

ISBN 0 7537 0635 0

Produced by Toppan (HK) Ltd

Printed in China

Cover Pictures: (1) a Steiff rod teddy bear, German, c.1904,
£10,000–12,000; (2) a Jumeau bébé, French, c.1880,
£4,000–5,000; (3) a George II wooden doll, English,
c.1750, £15,000–25,000; (4) Barbie doll, American,
c.1965, £300–500; (5) A Merythought
teddy bear, English, c.1935, £500–800.
picture pages 2 & 3 (from left to right): a Steiff brown
plush teddy bear, c.1908, £5,000–7000; a Circle and
Dot bisque doll, French, c.1875, £15,000–20,000;
a Bähr & Pröschild bisque character boy doll, c.1912,
£3,000–4,000; a fine and rare Emile Jumeau triste bisque
doll, French, c.1875, £7,000–9,000; a J.D. Kestner
bisque character doll, c.1910, £7,000–9,000;
a shoulder-china doll, German, c.1840, £4,000–6,000;
a Steiff 1913 golly, £4,000–6,000; a German papier-
mâché doll, c.1840, £600–800; a large long white
plush Steiff teddy bear, c.1920, £3,000–4,000;
a George II wooden doll, c.1740, £7,000–9,000;
a German teddy bear, maker uncertain, c.1908,
£2,000–4,000; Barbie and Ken, c.1965, for the
pair with box £500–800; a German wooden
doll, c.1850, £2,500–4,000.

CONTENTS

FOREWORD

Perhaps surpisingly, given my present career, dolls and teddy bears were not a major part of my childhood. My first recollection of playthings was a soft, cloth rabbit called Bunny and I adamantly adopted the name at age two when my parents bought me a wonderful fur coat with a hood and long ears. I refused to answer to another name (but my father was allowed to call me Bundle).

It seems that I was always outside and enjoying the delights of the garden. As soon as I could walk, my father taught me not to be afraid of any animals, birds or insects. I would bravely hold out my finger covered in strawberry jam to feed the wasps – or I was busy rescuing snakes or lizards or toads from the lawnmower. I also remember trying to resuscitate baby birds which had fallen from their nests or newborn, pink hedgehogs – which we fed with warm milk through a pipette.

Nature of all kinds was my passion and there was seldom a day when some poor creature was not to be found in a box in my bedroom or the garden shed. Birds, their nests and eggs held a fascination for me and horses also played a part of my later childhood.

When my adult senses began to mature, music and art appreciation made their appearance in the form of a job, first in an Oxford modern art gallery and then at Sotheby's main reception counter. People from every walk of life, from opera singers to tramps, brought in all manner of objects to be valued by the relevant expert. It was both a fascinating and instructive job and widened my interests further.

The Furniture Department was my next job and it was there that I felt completely at home. Antique furniture, and especially that which is English pre-Victorian, will always be my first love. In the 1960s, the furniture catalogues curiously included dolls and automata. I shall be eternally grateful to Charles Walford for encouraging my interest and teaching me not only about English furniture but also about dolls.

By the mid-1970s, I started studying dolls more seriously and to me they were never to be regarded simply as toys. The part they have played in our social history fascinates me, with

their clothes showing us the fashions and idealized notions of beauty which tend to vary from age to age. Seventeenth-century adult dress is rarely found even in museums so some wooden dolls are able to give us a valuable insight into the materials and styles which were used.

In 1980, more and more dolls were appearing for auction but were still being included in the furniture catalogues. It was then that I was invited to start a separate department at Sotheby's devoted exclusively to dolls and automata.

The first dolls' sale was particularly exciting for me because of a photograph of a doll which was sent from our Torquay saleroom. This led me to discover the doll's importance. I insisted that it be sent to Bond Street for auction and the French character Jumeau mould No. 203 was the star lot in my first doll sale of 1981. At auction, it realized an impressive £6,600!

There is a strange background to my current absorption which I find rather difficult to explain rationally. Many years before I knew anything about dolls or even what they were made of, a fortune-teller made the prediction that I would have a successful career surrounded by porcelain faces which were three-dimensional, not flat like plates. Neither he nor I could imagine what the image meant or the significance of it at the time. I had forgotten all about the prediction until, in 1980, I found myself in a cupboard with shelves full of bisque and porcelain dolls all staring at me. It was then that his words came flooding back!

The 1980s saw a boom in the doll market. In 1985, a new world record of £17,000 was achieved at Sotheby's for a William and Mary wooden doll. Two years later at the same saleroom, a similar doll made by the same craftsman and from the same period reached a staggering £64,000. Almost every consecutive year saw a new world auction record for a doll. In 1986, a German Kämmer and Reinhardt mould No.106 bisque doll of 1909 made £20,000, followed by a mould No.105 which made another record of £90,000 in 1989 (all at Sotheby's).

In 1993, a telephone call out of the blue set me on a course which was to establish a new world record for any doll. My reputation was at stake and my expertise severely tested when I was able to authenticate a unique Kämmer and Reinhardt bisque doll, mould No. 108, which the manufacturers had formally registered in Germany in 1909 but which experts did not know still existed. Imagine the nervousness I experienced as the sale day at Sotheby's approached. Fortunately, my conviction was vindicated by no less than three bidders (two in the saleroom and one on the telephone) who took the bidding well above the reserve to a staggering record level of £188,000!

The television film Brideshead Revisited was partly responsible for me deciding to hold the first-ever auction anywhere of teddy bears at Sotheby's in 1982. The actor Peter Bull, who had a large collection of bears and who also wrote a book about them, was my other great influence. He had lent his delightful 'Aloysius' to the BBC to use as Sebastian Flyte's famous teddy. (The bear had originally started life with the name 'Delicatessen' because he had been found lying on a shelf in a delicatessen shop.)

I was further influenced to hold the first sale by one of my doll clients who asked me if I would auction her collection of teddy bears. I fell in love with a black bear in that first-ever teddy auction. He turned out to be an American bear by the Ideal Toy Company but I didn't recognize this at the time. The sale was a raging success and the adorable bear which caught my heart sold for the first-ever teddy bear auction record of £460.

Media coverage of that first sale persuaded more and more people to sell their bears. The second auction record for a teddy bear was even more memorable for me as we achieved £2,100 for a 27-in (69-cm) beige Steiff of 1908 wearing a broderie-anglaise dress. She had been entered for sale by a family who had not one but two children with cystic fibrosis and the proceeds were helping to provide some life-giving equipment for them. The estimate had been that the bear would raise only £500–700 – so the job of telephoning the parents with such a good result was especially rewarding for me.

Each year saw a new record. There were the two Steiff silver plush muzzled bears which made £8,800 and the rod-jointed apricot plush Steiff

which realized £12,000 in 1987. In 1989 the world record was £60,000 for a 1928 Steiff gold plush bear and by early 1996 the world record stood at £110,000 paid by a Japanese for a Steiff 'Teddy Girl'. The interest in teddy bears continues to grow and it is difficult to imagine where these tremendous price levels will end.

The question I am always asked is what to look for when buying old dolls and bears. My advice is always to buy what you like. What you like is often what other people are likely to want as well. Generally, the most crucial factors which help to determine the price of dolls are their prettiness, originality and condition. Not surprisingly, rarity and price tend to go hand in hand.

As you never know when a remarkable find may come your way, be prepared. I always carry a pocket magnifying glass which is invaluable for an incredible range of uses. It will also guide you to seeing whether there is some tiny defect that you should be aware of before you make a purchase – such as a flaw in a doll's glass eye!

This book Collecting Teddy Bears and Dolls spans three centuries of dolls and also the development of bears and some other soft toys in more recent years. It takes the reader through all stages of collecting and is an absolutely invaluable guide for both beginners and seasoned collectors alike. Tips show you what to look for when you buy – and there is useful advice about fakes and forgeries.

The price guidelines should help you to gain some idea of value and why some bears and dolls are considered to be worth more than others. It may be surprising that even some fairly recent dolls and bears are already proving to be very good collectables. I only wish a book like this had been available to me back in the 1970s!

BUNNY CAMPIONE

The values given in this book for featured objects reflect the sort of prices you might expect to pay for similar pieces at an auction house or from a dealer. As there are so many variable factors involved in the pricing of antiques, the values should be used only as a general guide.

PERIODS & STYLES

Dates	British Monarchs	British Period	French Period	German Kaiser
1760–1811	George III	Georgian	Louis XVI (1774–93)	Karl VII (Wittelsbacher) (1742–1745)
			Directoire (1793–99)	1745 Franz I
				Joseph II (1765–1790)
				Leopold II (1790–1792)
			Empire (1799–1815)	Franz II (1792–1806)
1812–1820	George III	Regency	Restauration (1815–30) Charles X (1820–1830)	
1820–1830	George IV	Regency		
1830–1837	William IV	William IV	Louis Philippe (1830–48)	1848–Revolution
1837–1901	Victoria	Victorian	Second Empire (1852–70)	
			Third Republic (1871–1940)	Kaiser Wilhelm I (1871–1888)
				Kaiser Wilhelm II 1888–1918
1901–1910	Edward VII	Edwardian		Ausrufen der Republik 1918
1910–1936	George V			
1936–1952	George VI			
1952–	Elizabeth II			

German Period	US Period	Style	Type of Doll/Bear
Neo-classicism (1750–1800)	Early Federal (1790–1810)	Neo-classical (1755–1805)	Wooden English dolls Wax crèche figures from Italy Papier-mâché dolls from Germany Grödnertal pegged wooden dolls
Empire (1800–15)	American Directoire (1798–1804) American Empire (1804–15)	Empire (1799–1815)	
Biedermeier (1815–48 and 1880–1920)	Later Federal (1810–30)	Regency (1812–30)	Early wax dolls Papier-mâché China dolls
Revivale (1830–80)		Eclectic (1830–80)	First bisque dolls Wax and waxed composition dolls China-headed dolls First fashion dolls Cloth dolls First celluloid dolls
	Victorian		
Jugendstil (1880–1920)		Arts & Crafts (1880–1900)	
	Art Nouveau (1890–1920)	Art Nouveau (1890–1920)	Cloth dolls Composition dolls Teddy bears from 1903
			Ideal, Steiff 1920–30: Deans, Chad Valley, Merrythought, Bruin 1930- Bruin, Hermann, Schuco, cloth, Action Man, Sindy, Barbie, plastic and hard vinyl

PART 1

BUYING & SELLING

TEDDY BEARS & DOLLS

ABOVE A STEIFF TEDDY BEAR, C.1908. £4,000–6,000

LEFT A CABINET FULL OF DOLLS ON VIEW AT A
SOTHEBY'S DOLL AND TEDDY BEAR AUCTION.

STARTING A COLLECTION

A collection of bears or dolls often begins by chance. You are loath to throw away an old friend and so a treasured doll or bear goes through life with you and sits in a corner of your bedroom until a friend or lover presents you with another as a token of affection. Before long you spot a third in an antique shop looking lonely on a shelf, and in a short time you have become a collector.

The great appeal of collecting dolls is universal. Dolls were among the earliest toys, existing in every civilization from the most primitive to that of the present day. In contrast, the teddy bear is a very recent phenomenon. But the teddy bear's popularity is similarly unbounded, confined to no particular race or creed and welcoming each new owner with open arms and an unconditional love.

Both kinds of toys can provide an endearing and sometimes heart-rending insight into the lives of children of the past. Besides being

> ## SOME COLLECTORS
> - THE ANCIENT EGYPTIANS ARE THE FIRST KNOWN DOLL COLLECTORS
> - COL. BOB HENDERSON HELPED TO FOUND GOOD BEARS OF THE WORLD TO HELP SICK CHILDREN
> - ACTOR AND COLLECTOR PETER BULL LENT 'DELICATESSEN' TO PLAY 'ALOYSIUS' IN *BRIDESHEAD REVISITED* ON TELEVISION

objects of adoration or comfort they provided a means of role-playing in preparation for adult life. Making clothes for them was also a way of both practising sewing skills and learning about fashion.

Dolls especially offer an insight into social history, most notably the changes that have taken place during the 19th and 20th centuries. Ideals of beauty are reflected in different shapes of doll as well as their clothes and hairstyles. An idealization of children is seen in the 19th-century French bébés when dolls and their wardrobes became status symbols, a measure of the parent's affluence.

In the 20th century a more realistic approach took over with German character dolls. Bears as well as dolls began to show the influence of films and television on children. The publication of popular children's books worldwide has led to the most unexpected characters, such as Pooh and Paddington, becoming household names.

Once collecting has become a conscious decision, it can take a multitude of forms. At one extreme are those who feel they must collect strictly by type and date, amassing every bear or doll of one particular make or period. At the other extreme are the eclectic collectors who buy something just because it takes their fancy. Whatever kind of collector you are, you will probably get at least as much excitement out of the hunt for a doll or bear and its identification as in its ownership.

The first decision is to work out what you can afford, although most collectors say that the bears or dolls they love best are the ones they bought regardless, when the purchase was simply an irresistible impulse. The most valuable ones such as 17th-century wooden dolls and early Steiff bears now change hands for tens of thousands

Snow White complete with her seven dwarfs, made in England by Chad Valley c.1935. £2,000–3,000

This French Jumeau-type bisque doll was produced by the Société Française de Fabrication de Bébés et Jouets (S.F.B.J.) c.1907. £1,000–1,500

of pounds or more. But only a few pounds are necessary to begin a collection if you look for the antiques of the future, such as 1980s soft-toy Power Rangers. Even less outlay is involved if you have any old Disney characters, for instance, hidden in an attic.

The cheapest places to buy are likely to be markets or junk shops or general auctions. But even the smartest salerooms or antique shops may have a bargain if you have done your homework. The first rule is do not be afraid to ask questions. The second is do not be deterred if you make a mistake. Top collectors do, only they keep quiet about it. An error can turn out to be the best way to learn.

Decide also how you feel about the condition of a doll or bear. With both toys, subject to the affections of perhaps generations of children, condition can affect the price very dramatically. So you could buy a relatively rare example for a small sum if you do not mind missing fur or fingers. On the other hand, if you want a sumptuous purchase but cannot afford a big name, look for a similar item by a lesser known or even unidentified producer. Dotting teddy bears and dolls around your

home is like adding to your family. Moreover the age and style of your house need not make any difference to what you collect, as it would if you were buying decorative art or furniture. Old dolls can look exquisite in contemporary or period furnishings. Teddy bears and other soft toys can give a homely feel to any surroundings. But beware of heat, light and moths and visitors who have dogs or small children. Central heating dries the air so much that wooden or wax dolls may crack. Sunlight may cause skin colours as well as dress materials to fade. Fur is especially vulnerable to hungry insects and any doll or bear is likely to be attractive to small fingers and worrying teeth.

On the following pages are pointers to help you to select and purchase your investment. But above all, buy what you really feel you cannot do without. Then eventually, should you decide to sell your collection, or just to upgrade it, you will find that someone else will probably fall in love with your bears and dolls just as you did. The result is a profit to yourself along with years of pleasure from your collection.

While the maker is uncertain, this is clearly a much-loved English bear showing wear from hugs and cuddles. It dates from about 1935. £200–300

AUCTIONS

In recent years antique dolls and teddy bears have leapt out of the nursery and attic and into the media with tales of record-breaking prices. Although these news stories make fascinating reading, they will tend to give inexperienced buyers the very misleading impression that only dolls and bears which are worth thousands of pounds are ever sold at auction, when in fact these sales are very much the exceptional ones.

Even the great head-line-hogging West End auction houses sell many more of the modestly priced dolls and bears than they sell expensive ones, and throughout Britain there is an enormous number of small provincial auction houses holding regular sales at which all types of doll and bear are bought and sold.

Many new collectors are rather daunted at the prospect of visiting an auction house for the first time, but if you follow just a few simple guidelines, going to auctions can prove a very affordable way of buying and selling dolls and bears, and it is much more fun than buying conventionally.

> **BUYING AT AUCTION CHECKLIST**
> - STUDY THE CATALOGUE
> - REGISTER YOUR DETAILS BEFORE BIDDING
> - DECIDE ON YOUR LIMIT AND STICK TO IT

ATTENDING A SALE

A few days before a sale takes place, the dolls and bears will be put on view to the public. It is important to make the effort to view the auction properly beforehand. Do not expect to be able to view the various dolls and bears immediately prior to the auction, as the porters will often be rearranging the lots ready for collection after the sale. Buying 'on spec' is usually a mistake too, so be careful.

It is always worth buying a catalogue to refer to when looking at the view. At larger salerooms the catalogue entry for each 'lot' (item in the sale) gives you a fairly detailed description of each piece, including the date it was made, the maker and a note of any damage or alterations. These auction houses also offer a conditional guarantee of authenticity, so if something described as 18th century turns out to be a later copy you do have some recourse.

Most catalogues include estimated prices too. This gives you a good idea of what the auction house expects the piece to fetch at the sale, based on prices realized for similar objects. The estimates are useful as general guides, but do not expect them to be 100 per cent accurate. There are always surprises depending on the competition for a particular piece on the day – and this is part of the thrill of buying at auction.

Although catalogues are invaluable, there is no better way to learn about dolls and teddy bears than by handling them. When you view a sale, make sure you examine the pieces you are interested in as closely as possible. For instance, check for cracks in the head of bisque-headed dolls, make sure the clothing is original and, with bears, make sure the maker's label is still there if it should have one, check the condition of the 'fur' carefully too.

Going, going, gone...a Christie's auction of teddy bears.

Dolls and teddy bears are often sold along with automata and toys. This collection awaits auction at Sotheby's.

If you are uncertain about something, ask to speak to the expert in charge, who will probably be able to give you more information on the piece than was contained in the description. You can also ask for a condition report (a detailed analysis on an individual lot) which is available free of charge.

BIDDING AND BUYING

Before you can bid in an auction you must register with the auction house accounts department (giving your name, address and possibly bank details). Many salerooms will then issue you with a 'paddle' number, a card with a number on it that you show to the auctioneer should your bid be successful.

Many people bidding for the first time at auction are terrified at the prospect of simply coughing and landing themselves with a very expensive, perhaps unwanted, item. In fact, this is almost impossible as an auctioneer is trained to spot bidders. Once he or she knows you are interested, he or she will glance back to you to see if you want to continue to bid.

If you are the successful bidder, the auctioneer will knock the gavel down at the price reached. He will then ask for your 'paddle' number which will be written down in the 'auctioneer's book' as a confirmation of sale. This process signifies a legally binding contract so you cannot decide to change your mind after the gavel has fallen.

Keep in mind also that on top of the final hammer price (the price at which the bidding stops) you will have to pay the auction house a premium (which is usually between 10 and 15 per cent), as well as VAT on the premium. If there is a dagger symbol or an asterisk by the catalogue description, then be sure to read the conditions of sale section carefully as these symbols usually mean added VAT.

ABSENTEE BIDS

If you are unable to attend the auction you can leave a bid with the absentee bids office and for no extra charge the commissions clerk or auctioneer will bid on your behalf. If you are undecided between two lots, you can leave

A selection of Lenci dolls from a Sotheby's sale.

'either or' bids; in other words you instruct the clerk to buy either, say, lot 52, or, if unsuccessful, lot 75. The commissions clerk is bound to purchase for you as inexpensively as possible. Nevertheless, it is always best to attend the sale yourself.

PAYING AND COLLECTING

Make sure that you know the auction house requirements for payment and collection before you buy. Most auction houses expect you to pay and collect your furniture within a limited period of time (usually five working days) and will charge interest and storage if you fail to do so. Many auction houses accept major credit cards as well as a cheque or cash.

If you buy an item (or a number of items) too big to take home yourself the auction house will usually recommend a carrier, although they rarely have their own delivery services. You will be responsible for any transport costs you incur.

SELLING AT AUCTION

There is usually no charge for an over-the-counter valuation for a doll or bear and you are not committed to sell afterwards if you do not want to. If you decide to sell, keep in mind that an auction house, unlike a dealer, does not buy your property from you, it sells it on your behalf. For this service you will probably be charged a commission of between 10 and 15 per cent on the hammer price, together with VAT on the commission, an insurance charge and a handling charge. Christie's and Sotheby's have a sliding scale of charges, depending on the volume of business you consign. If your property is going to be illustrated in the auction catalogue you will be charged an additional fee to cover the costs of photography. In the unlikely event of your

bear or doll not selling, there may well be charges, albeit reduced.

In the larger auction houses, specialist sales of teddy bears and dolls occur only every few months, so you may have to wait some time for your money. Also, if the piece is particularly special, the auction house may suggest it is put into one of their 'good' sales which attract their top clients. These generally occur once or twice a year.

RESERVE PRICES

If the items you are selling are worth more than £500, the saleroom will probably advise you to put a reserve price on it. This is a safeguard so that if the auction is poorly attended, your priceless property will not sell for £50. The reserve price given is usually fixed at the bottom estimate or between 10 and 15 per cent below this figure.

Bunny Campione, Sotheby's consultant for teddy bears and dolls, discusses a Steiff teddy bear with a client.

ANTIQUES & JUNK SHOPS

The golden rule when buying dolls and teddy bears from antiques shops is to go only to a reputable dealer. This means a dealer who is a member of a recognized trade association. In Britain the two main bodies are LAPADA (which is the London and Provincial Antiques Dealers Association), and BADA (British Antiques Dealers'Association). In the US it is the Art & Antiques Dealers' League of America.

If you buy from a member of a recognized trade association this will protect you in several ways. In order to join the association, the dealer will have had to demon-strate a sound knowledge of his subject. His stock will have been assessed to be of good quality and the dealer will have to abide by a strict code of practice that requires him to display prices openly, to describe his stock accurately and to deal fairly with his customers. Another advantage of buying from a good dealer is that if

Teddy Bears of Witney, Oxfordshire, and owner Ian Pout.

you find you get on well with him or her you might build up a long-lasting relationship that will benefit both of you. The dealer might look out for special pieces for you that are not in stock, or offer to buy back pieces he or she has sold to you so that you can upgrade your collection.

BUYING FROM A DEALER CHECKLIST

- PICK A REPUTABLE DEALER
- COMPARE PRICES FOR SIMILAR PIECES IN OTHER SHOPS
- FIND OUT WHAT, IF ANY, RESTORATION HAS BEEN CARRIED OUT
- TAKE YOUR TIME WHEN CHOOSING WHAT TO BUY
- GET A DETAILED RECEIPT

BUYING FROM A DEALER

Once you have found a good dealer and spotted something you want to buy in his or her shop, ask for as much information as possible. The doll or bear will probably carry a label stating the maker and date, but the dealer will probably be able to expand on the item too. Ask if there is an interest-ing history, or prove-nance, to the piece and if any restoration or repair has been carried out. When it comes to agreeing the price there are no hard and fast rules but in many antiques shops the first fig-ure you are quoted is not the 'best' price and if you 'discuss' the sum you will often find that you can reduce it a little.

Once you have paid for the doll or bear, make sure you are given a detailed receipt which should include the dealer's name, the date, price and clear description of the object, including the approximate date it was made.

SELLING TO A DEALER

If you are thinking of selling a bear or doll through a dealer, make sure you choose a spe-cialist in these fields rather than a general antiques shop where dolls and bears will be overshadowed by other objects. It is a good idea to telephone first to check whether or not the dealer is interested in what you wish to sell, or even to send a photograph. As a result, some dealers may come to you.

Selling to a dealer has several advantages. The price you agree is the sum you will receive – there are no hidden deductions such as insurance and VAT, and you will be given your money immediately. However, if you are trying to sell an item after it has failed to sell at auction and the dealer recognizes it, he or she is less likely to buy it from you as it is no longer 'fresh' to the market. Also, decide initially whether you are prepared to leave your doll or bear on a 'sale or return' basis, as some dealers operate this way. If you do hand over your property, make sure you are given a receipt which includes its value and a description of the condition of the doll or bear in case it is damaged.

CLUBS

Some teddy-bear dealers operate specialist collectors' clubs for certain makes such as Dean's or Steiff. These clubs can provide a wealth of detailed information and up-to-date values. The same dealers often also run a hospital service for sick bears.

'KNOCKERS'

Never sell to people who simply turn up uninvited at your home or put a note through the door offering to call back later and buy your unwanted old furniture and other objects. Many of these so-called 'knockers' are highly disreputable people and will try to trick you into parting with your personal property for much less than it is worth.

JUNK SHOPS

Most junk shops find their stock from house clearance sales and deceased properties where the entire contents are bought for a fixed sum. Thus, you will find an enormous variety of different types of objects for sale, usually for relatively inexpensive prices. The best items will have already been sold on by the shop owner, but, if you have a keen eye, these places can be fruitful sources of inexpensive collectables. Sometimes a scruffy-looking bear or doll may be overlooked by the dealers and end up in the junk shop but, realistically, you are more likely to find a Sindy than a Steiff

The range of bears and dolls in shops is wonderful but can be bewildering. Decide what you like best and build your collection gradually from that.

here. Sindys, however, can be valuable (see pages 160–61) so this is when it pays off to have done your homework and to know exactly what you are looking at. The golden rule is of course not to let on just how interested you are – otherwise you may find that the price suddenly goes up.

FAIRS, MARKETS & PERSONAL SALES

Antiques fairs have proliferated in recent years, as have specialist doll fairs and teddy-bear fairs. Now they are one of the most popular ways to buy antiques and collectables. Each year hundreds take place in Britain alone as well as in continental Europe and the United States and most dealers, realizing their potential, take stands at one or more events. Some do not have a shop but deal only privately except at certain fairs where they seek to build up their clientele.

The larger fairs are likely to have specialist stalls of antique dolls and teddy bears. They may also have collectable modern dolls such as Barbie along with Steiff replica bears. Such fairs are a good opportunity to compare stock and prices under one roof, select what you like best and decide who is offering the best deal. You will probably be charged an entry fee to such a fair and be given a catalogue with a list of exhibitors. This is a useful source of reference since it will not merely give the stand numbers of exhibitors but also their business addresses and telephone numbers. Dealers are usually only too pleased to chat about their stock in the hope that even if you do not buy you may visit them after the fair.

> ## BUYING CHECKLIST AT FAIRS & MARKETS
> - GET THERE EARLY
> - CARRY A TORCH
> - TAKE CASH IF YOU PLAN TO BUY
> - TRY TO GET A RECEIPT

VETTING

The added safeguard of larger fairs is that all the exhibitors will have been invited to take part because of their good reputation and the quality of their stock. Each exhibit will have been 'vetted' which means that it will have been examined by a panel of independent experts. These are usually auction-house valuers, museum curators and specialist dealers who make sure the item is authentic and has not been over-restored. Some fairs, however, operate a dateline which means that nothing made after say 1900 may be exhibited which, of course, rules out bears.

Smaller fairs are some of the best places to find a bargain. Numerous such fairs, specialist and otherwise, take place throughout the country. There may be a small entry fee but goods will be less expensive and the exhibitors may not have the same degree of expertise. Here is the chance to make your own mind up about age and authenticity without having to risk a fortune.

MARKETS

Antiques markets are on a par with the smaller fairs although some, such as Portobello Road in London and the Flea Market (Marché aux Puces) in Paris, have become established tourist attractions. They usually take place on only one or two days a week and you need to arrive very early if you are after a bargain. Keep in mind, however, that if you do part with a large sum of money you may not have the same recourse as if you had bought from a recognized dealer, and markets are a favourite

A 1936 Teddy Tail's Annual.

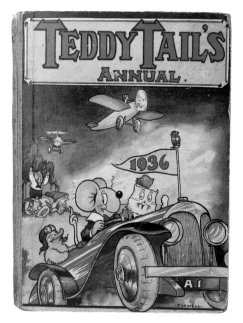

This Stacey bag may be valuable in the future.

place for disposing of stolen property. Get a receipt, as from a shop, if you possibly can.

BOOT SALES

Generally held in farmers' fields, school playgrounds or large car parks, boot sales are advertised in local newspapers, the classified columns of certain magazines and on notices pinned to trees or lamp-posts. Some are very regular events, some one-offs. Anything can be sold at a boot sale, so equally anything could turn up. A 1980s Power Ranger could be a good bet for the future or a less obvious item from the Barbie range might appear, relating to one of her friends such as Stacey.

SELLING AT BOOT SALES

You may be charged an entrance fee according to the size of your vehicle. You need to get there early to get a prime position and set yourself up properly. It is a good idea to pack the car the night before, checking as you do that everything you want to take fits in. Mark or decide how much you will want for your property as this will save you time and panic when you get there.

BUYING FROM ADVERTISEMENTS

National and local newspapers as well as more specialist magazines carry classified advertisements. Avoid a wasted trip by finding out as much as you can about the item and its state of repair before you journey to see it.

SELLING THROUGH ADVERTISEMENTS

Be sure you have a sound idea of the market value of your doll or bear before placing an advertisement. The best way is to sound the opinion of a few dealers or auction specialists. Word the advertisement as clearly and succinctly as you can, including any point that could make the item attractive to a buyer. Include a box number or telephone number but for security do not include your name or address. Make certain that you are available to answer the telephone when your advertisement appears and be prepared to name a price and give a full description and condition report on the item. Negotiate if necessary but never part with your property until you have been paid in full, preferably in cash.

Relatively recently made items, such as this Barbie set, are more likely to be found at fairs or markets.

PART 2

TEDDY BEAR &

DOLL CARE

ABOVE AN ENGLISH 1950S BEAR IN A
19TH-CENTURY CARVED WOODEN DOLL'S BED.
£500–700 FOR THE TWO

LEFT (LEFT TO RIGHT, BACK ROW) A STEIFF BEAR,
1908, £4,000–6,000; A BRU JEUNE BISQUE DOLL,
FRENCH, C.1891, £3,000–5,000; A STEIFF BEAR,
1910, £2,000–3,000; (FRONT ROW) A JUMEAU
BISQUE DOLL, FRENCH, 1885, £2,500–3,000; A
GERMAN 'MASK-FACE' GOOGLY COMPOSITION DOLL,
C.1910, £500–700; A STEINER BISQUE DOLL,
FRENCH, C.1895, £2,000–3000

VALUING, INSURING & SECURITY

No keen collector enjoys contemplating the loss of a prized possession but, unfortunately, an unpleasant aspect of collecting antiques today is the growing risk of burglary. One result of the increasing number of art and antiques thefts is that most insurance companies now demand a professional written valuation to cover objects which are worth more than a certain amount.

If you are just starting out as a teddy-bear or doll collector you will certainly have a fair idea what each piece is worth and whether you need a valuation. But supposing you bought them a decade or more ago, do you really know what they are worth and for what sums they should be insured? In recent years, many types of doll and bear have risen dramatically in value. Numerous dolls and bears that were once modestly valued are now worth substantial sums, so if you are unsure as to the value of your collection and whether you need to have a valuation, it is a good idea to take some professional advice. Although a valuation will inevitably involve some expense, if the property is not valued you could find that in the event of any burglary or accident you are inadequately insured and unable to replace your property.

SECURITY CHECKLIST

- **MAKE YOUR HOME UNINVITING TO BURGLARS**
- **TAKE EXTRA PRECAUTIONS WHEN YOU ARE AWAY ON HOLIDAY**
- **PHOTOGRAPH EVERYTHING OF VALUE IN YOUR COLLECTION, BUT DO NOT KEEP THE PHOTOGRAPHS IN YOUR HOME**
- **KEEP AN UPDATED INVENTORY OF YOUR COLLECTION**

VALUATIONS

There are various ways you can arrange to have your antiques valued. If you know some friendly dealer and have only a few items, he or she may be able to provide a valuation, although you should check with your insurance company that this will be acceptable. If you have a fairly extensive collection, your insurance company may prefer a valuation from a specialist valuer or one of the larger auction houses, all of whom have valuation departments.

One of the main advantages of using an auction house is that the specialist will have a wide breadth of experience in the field, accumulated by handling all types of bear or doll every day. He or she will also have an acute commercial awareness gained from holding regular auctions and keeping an eye on sales taking place at rival auction houses. If you have only a few bears to be valued you should take them into the auction house. The specialist will be able to offer you a free verbal valuation on the spot and there is no need to make an appointment. If you need to have the valuation for insurance purposes, you will be charged a fee (see opposite) and if you have a large collection, a representative of the auction house will come to visit you.

BACK (left to right): Simon and Halbig bisque character doll, mould No.151, German 1912, 17¾in (46cm), £5,000; Kämmer & Reinhardt, mould No. 1078, German, 1892, £600.
FRONT (left to right): Kämmer & Reinhardt closed-mouth bisque doll, mould No. 117. £4,000–5,000; a Kämmer & Reinhardt bisque doll, mould No. 117N (with open mouth). £1,000–1,500

You may be surprised to learn exactly what you own. One elderly woman who was blind had a doll with four interchangeable heads and thought it might be worth £100 or so. Sotheby's sold it for £6,000 and the proceeds enabled her to buy a flat. Another woman who had paid £5 for a doll she liked in a car boot sale decided she had better sell it when she was told she had a Bru Jeune of 1875. She was giving her children tea when she was telephoned by Sotheby's with the result. On hearing that it had been sold for £16,500, she collapsed on the table.

THE COST OF VALUING

Valuations can be costly, so before you decide whom to call in to value your property, shop around and look for the best deal. Prices vary and can be calculated either as a percentage of the total value of your property (usually between ½ and 1½ percent, on a daily rate, or as an agreed flat rate. Generally, a valuer will be able to assess between 100 and 300 pieces a day depending on the detail required.

To some extent the fee you are quoted for your valuation will depend upon how much the auction house wishes to secure you as a client. To an auction house, a valuation is recognized as being an important way of establishing loyalty with their firm. So the chances are that if you have an extensive collection of, say, Steiff bears, the auction house will be keen to lure you to their firm and may be prepared to negotiate. You should always make sure you agree the final figure before the valuation takes place rather than afterwards. Some auction houses offer an added bonus by reducing their commission rates should you decide to sell any of the items they have valued within a reasonably short period of time.

Whoever carries out your valuation, you should make sure that it includes a full description of every item, together with its dimensions and value for insurance purposes. The value placed upon each object will to some extent depend on where you would go to replace your property: would you go to a

A Bru Jeune bisque doll, French, c.1880. £15,000–20,000

top London dealer or to your local auction house? The price an insurance valuer puts on your property will probably be at least 20 per cent higher than what you could expect to get should you decide to sell. If you feel this will make your insurance premiums prohibitively high, you can opt for a 'market' valuation – in other words auction price – instead. But keep in mind that if the valuation is too low, you could find yourself unable to replace any lost items satisfactorily.

INSURING

The person you choose to insure your antiques may be able to advise you on a suitable insurer. One way of reducing premiums is to shop around. If your collection is moderately large and valuable you will probably find it is less expensive to insure it through a broker specializing in art and antiques, rather than through a general insurer. Whereas a large insurer will usually lump together your antiques in the general household policy, a specialist broker will assess the risk of different categories of antique individually, therefore reducing premiums. Unfortunately, dolls and teddy bears are small and portable items and as such are more expensive to insure than large pieces such as furniture.

SECURITY

Teddy bears and dolls are a burglar's dream: light and portable, they can be bundled away in seconds. Therefore it is particularly important for collectors to take extra precautions. First, you should try to deter potential thieves from entering your home by making it as secure as possible. If you are unsure about how to go about this, you can contact the crime prevention officer through your local police station. He or she will advise you on safeguarding your belongings and can also recommend reputable security firms in your area to install additional locks or alarms or whatever other equipment may be necessary.

But what if disaster should strike and you do find yourself the victim of crime? By far the best way of helping the police is to provide them with as much information about your stolen property as possible. An inventory or list of your collection will be invaluable (see below), but it is also vitally important to have a clear photograph of each object in your collection.

Photographs of any stolen antiques can be logged via your local police officer with the Art and Antiques Squad at Scotland Yard. This police department has a national database which contains descriptions and photographic images of works of art stolen throughout the country. When stolen property is recovered, the Art and Antiques Squad can identify the rightful owner – provided that the object has been logged onto their computer system. But you do need a photograph to stand a good chance of recovery. It is salutary to remember that the vast majority of stolen antiques the police recover are never claimed. In such cases, not only does the culprit evade any

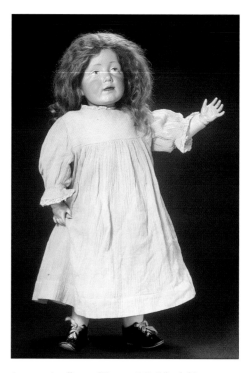

An exceptionally rare Kämmer & Reinhardt bisque character doll, c.1909. £90,000–100,000

prosecution, but the property is actually returned to him or her! By photographing your property you will be helping to redress this balance and increase the chance of your recovering stolen items.

PHOTOGRAPHING

You may want to enlist the help of a professional photographer to photograph your collection, although if you observe a few simple guidelines it is quite a simple task to do it yourself. It is best to photograph objects using colour film outdoors in natural daylight. Choose a day when there is a light cloud cover so that the sunlight is not too harsh and the shadows not very noticeable. For the clearest results, you can either use standard 35mm 100ASA print film or the new, specially improved Polaroid camera. The older type of Polaroids are not very satisfactory long-term photographic records as the colours can be unstable and fade.

The new Polaroid cameras are available on free loan from the Crime Prevention Officers of many police stations, but you do have to supply your own film. To get the best results, stand with the sun behind you, stand level with the object, not above or to one side and close enough for the object to fill the viewfinder. If the objects are very small, photograph them against a plain background; white is usually the best colour for this unless the object itself is predominantly white, in which case use a grey or black background.

It is also useful when photographing your collection to include a scale reference and a ruler placed beside each object is a good way of doing this. If the object is behind glass, stand slightly to one side to avoid causing reflection and glare.

Take at least one shot of each object, as well as close-up shots of any identifying scratches, bumps or marks Photograph a doll both dressed and undressed, with special attention to the face. Take a close-up of any important features on a bear, such as a long snout.

As well as these individual photographs, it is also a good idea to take general shots of your room. These will help you to remember any smaller items. Keep photographs together in a safe place. Ideally, they should be filed with your inventory entry for each object. It is also a wise precaution to store a copy of photographs somewhere else for safekeeping – ideally with your bank or your solicitor.

DOCUMENTING

Documenting a collection means keeping a record of every collectable bear or doll as you acquire it. It is a good idea to keep your records of each item all together in an inventory book. Then as your collection grows you will find you have both a useful source of reference as well as an interesting reminder of how your collection began.

Keeping a detailed record of each object in your collection is also an ideal way to show proof of ownership in the event of an insurance claim. So any new purchase should be documented and photographed as soon as possible after you have brought it home.

To begin your inventory, make a list of every object you wish to include. Then for each object write down the following:

● Where it came from, and when.
● The price you paid for it.
● A full description of the piece, including its size, what it is made from and any decorative features.
● A report of its condition, including cracks, chips, alterations or restoration. This should be updated whenever you have the piece restored.
● Anything else you know about the doll's or teddy bear's history. Keep the receipts of anything you have purchased with the inventory.

A group of Schuco miniature bears and monkey. £200–300

DISPLAY & STORAGE

Contrast shows these two Steiff bears to best advantage.
Blonde: £3,000–4,000; black £12,000–18,000

Dolls and bears can be displayed in many ways but it is always important to choose a method of display that will be appropriate to your home and lifestyle.

Although bears and dolls need to be protected from such hazards as direct sunlight and damp, many people display their collections throughout their homes, perhaps surrounded by suitable accessories. However, if you have young children or pets, your collection would be safer in a cabinet out of harm's way.

There are several important factors to consider when choosing a place to display your dolls. Excessive central heating is detrimental to antique dolls, particularly those made from wax and wax-over-composition and wood. Dolls should never be displayed over a radiator or close to a direct source of heat; a fairly cool even temperature is ideal. Prolonged exposure to cigarette, pipe or cigar smoke can cause the dolls to discolour and will damage their clothes. If the doll comes with an original box, always keep this safe, even if you do not wish to display it, as it is very important to the value of the doll. Wax

or composition dolls should not be displayed in cabinets with overhead internal lighting, as this will melt them.

Purpose-made doll stands can be purchased by mail order through doll magazines or at specialist doll fairs. Some collectors display dolls by type, date, or other category. Mixing different types together can seem friendlier and more informal, or you can devise a more theatrical set piece.

Teddy bears require similar treatment to fabric dolls. They should be protected from sunlight and from dogs and young children. The eyes of old bears can be a particular source of danger, as many of them are attached by wires.

STORING DOLLS

If you are storing dolls away, make sure they are wrapped in acid-free tissues. Always lay them face down in boxes – as storing a doll with sleeping eyes on its back can result in the eyes jamming shut. Always avoid plastic bags and bubble-wrap. These can trap moisture over a period of time and this can cause damage to painted surfaces.

Lenci dolls, such as these 1920s Harlequins, were often made for display. £2,000–2,500 each

Colour co-ordination makes for a good display for Schmitt dolls. £6,000–8,000 each

STORING BEARS

The same rules apply as for storing dolls – use acid-free tissues and avoid plastic and bubble-wrap. Take care not to squash the bear while packing and beware of moths.

PACKING DOLLS

When packing a doll for travel, ensure that it is extremely well wrapped. Bisque-headed dolls, as well as those of wax and other media, should be protected with bubble-wrap, a disposable nappy or old towel to absorb any bumps or knocks sustained in transit. If the doll has bisque or wax limbs these should be separately and carefully wrapped.

PACKING BEARS

Unlike dolls, teddy bears are not breakable, but nevertheless they can fall apart. Wrap them carefully but not too tightly. Again, bubble-wrap or towelling are good shock absorbers. Avoid screwed-up newspaper unless the bear is first wrapped in something else, as the newsprint could leave marks.

PACKAGING

Dolls and bears can have several outfits. If these came in an original box or trunk, do not throw it away or exchange it for a smarter one. Even if it is not in the best condition, any original packaging of the doll or bear itself will add to the value.

Watch out for moths, however. A 19th-century French fashion trunk can be well worth displaying, but if it is left open and undisturbed then moths will be only too happy to make a meal of the contents – especially any delicious silk.

Putting tiny bears together can make them look even more impressive, while adding a small toy to a group or mixing dolls and bears together can give more characters to a scene. If you can display your bears and dolls around the house, be ingenious. Dress a bear in formal dinner suit to accompany a French fashion doll to supper. Give an inquisitive bear an old pair of spectacles and set him peering at a picture or reading a book. Or you could even sit a couple of bears in the bathroom, with one holding a flannel and the other holding a dish of soap.

A German doll, c.1910, complete with its original box. The box adds greatly to the doll's value. £1,500–2,000+

CARE & RESTORATION

In general, the less restoration a doll or teddy bear undergoes the better. However, certain types of doll are very susceptible to particular problems and may require limited restoration to prevent them from deteriorating further.

This section outlines some of the most common problems encountered with dolls of different media and teddy bears. Remember that bad restoration can cause irreversible damage and dramatically reduce the value of the doll or teddy bear. If in doubt, it is always best to check with a specialist dealer, auction house or museum first, particularly when dealing with costly or rare bears and dolls.

TEDDY BEARS

Restoration can be vitally important to the conservation of a teddy bear and, as with dolls, it is always best to consider carefully before doing anything. Dirty bears should be cleaned by a specialist; if they are left untreated the dirt can cause the fabric to rot. Holes in a bear can be mended without detracting from the bear's value. When patching, always try to use similar, preferably old, fabric, and leave as much of the original fabric as possible. Paw pads made from felt often suffer some damage so it is always much

This large 1880 Bru Jeune doll has brown, spiralled glass eyes, delicately tinted skin, an open-closed mouth, formed breasts and a signed kid-leather body. Although her original cutwork dress has been replaced in modern style and she has a new wig, she is still highly desirable because she is so timelessly attractive. £12,000–14,000

better to patch them than to replace them completely. How much the value of a bear may be affected by pad replacement varies considerably, so even if you think there is no alternative, it is better to check first.

BISQUE-HEADED DOLLS

Jointed dolls with bisque heads often have stringing which has perished, causing the doll to feel very floppy. It is important to handle such dolls with great care or the head may fall off and break. If possible, unhook the head and wrap it in tissue.

Dolls should be re-strung using special elastic to the right tension. If too tight, stringing can damage the doll's neck; too loose and the doll will not hold together. A local doll's hospital should be able to re-string a doll at relatively low cost.

Cracks are common in bisque-headed dolls. Such flaws require expert attention and are usually expensive to repair invisibly. If the doll is valuable it is worth having it well restored.

This 1908 Steiff gold plush bear is worn but worth £1,000–1,500, while this English 1950s bear is in good condition but worth only £200–300.

If it is an inexpensive doll it may be possible to disguise the crack with some hair brushed across the forehead. If the head is badly damaged you may consider replacing it with another similar one. In general, it is not advisable to disguise facial cracks by repainting as this looks unattractive and reduces the value of the doll. Most collectors prefer to see a few cracks and the original bisque.

Bisque heads can be cleaned by washing with cotton wool dipped in pure soap and water. It is vital to keep the water well away from the eyes, as it can either remove or loosen eyelashes and eyes.

Sleep eyes that are not in working order can be reset by an expert and teeth can be replaced. Fingers on composition bodies often need to be replaced; they can usually be effectively treated and do not detract from the overall value of the doll.

Composition bodies should not be washed as this will damage varnish and cause loss of colour and shine.

CHINA AND PARIAN DOLLS

China and parian heads can be washed with a damp cloth if necessary. Kid or leather bodies cannot be cleaned and are better left alone. Leaking sawdust can be patched with old kid gloves. Dolls with damaged cloth bodies can be patched using old fabric and shoulder-heads re-sewn or stuck back on.

Over-restoration has reduced the value of this 1800 English wooden doll. £700–900

WOODEN DOLLS

Wooden dolls are best left alone. If you are lucky enough to own an 18th-century doll, seek expert advice if it is damaged, as it requires highly specialized treatment. Never try to wash a wooden doll as this will remove the protective gesso and varnish.

WAX DOLLS

Dolls made of wax and also wax-over-composition/papier-mâché also require some specialist restoration. Although they are often cracked, these cracks are best left alone. Poured-wax dolls can be restored, although there are only a few specialists in this field.

FABRIC DOLLS

Fabrics dolls are very difficult to clean. Even 'washable' types should not be washed as this could ruin them. Bodies can be carefully patched and re-stitched and moth holes, which are particularly common on felt dolls, can be mended. If the face of a cloth doll is damaged, it is better left alone as you may damage it further by attempting restoration.

MODERN DOLLS

Newer dolls, such as those made from hard plastic and vinyl, must be in an excellent condition as collectors accept fewer blemishes than on old dolls. Never break into an unopened packet containing a doll or doll's clothes as doing so could halve their value.

WIGS

Wigs should be carefully treated. They often seem sparse, but where there is enough hair it should be teased out. A hat or bonnet can disguise stringy hair. Early fashion dolls with original hair should not be tampered with, but replacement wigs made from mohair or real hair are available for less-rare German and French child dolls.

Always keep the original wigs and clothing you replace and label them for future reference. Inspect the doll for wig pulls – which are small flakes of bisque that sometimes come away from the head when the wig is removed.

PART 3

TEDDY BEAR & DOLL
FUNDAMENTALS

ABOVE A ROD–JOINTED APRICOT STEIFF PLUSH
TEDDY BEAR FROM GERMANY, C.1904, WITH AN
ELEPHANT BUTTON. £12,000–18,000

LEFT THE FOUR INTERCHANGEABLE HEADS, IN
THEIR ORIGINAL BOX, OF A KESTNER BISQUE DOLL
MADE IN GERMANY C.1910. ALL HAVE THEIR
MOULD NUMBERS ON THE BACK. THE HEADS WITH
CLOSED MOUTHS ARE THE RARER CHARACTERS.
£6,000–8,000 INCLUDING THE BODY

DOLLS: MATERIALS & CONSTRUCTION

Knowledge of the materials used and the methods of construction of different types of doll is vital for assessing their authenticity and value. Although as a general rule dolls are classified by the material from which their head is made, the rest of the body may be composed of something completely different. Carefully fashioned hands and feet often give a clue to quality, although they are probably the most likely parts to have been replaced. The following pointers outline the basic details to remember.

WOOD

Early dolls were mostly made either from turned or carved wood in the wood-carving areas of Germany and Austria. In England wooden dolls were produced from the 17th century until the early 1900s. This one with missing arms is late-18th century. Later ones became very crude and were known simply as either 'Dutch dolls' or 'penny woodens'.

WAX

Wax was used by dollmakers from the 17th to the 20th centuries. The earliest were solid wax either carved or moulded. Poured-wax dolls, which were highly expensive, were made in the 19th century, mostly in England. Between 1830 and 1890, dolls were made from a moulded core of composition or papier-mâché dipped or painted with a layer of wax as a cheaper alternative. papier-mâché

Papier-mâché-headed dolls were introduced in Germany for commercial manufacture in 1800, although they had previously been made in a lesser way in France, England and elsewhere in Europe. The heads were made by pressing wet papier-mâché into moulds. When dry, the heads were painted, unusually in this case as a mulatto, and varnished. The essential ingredients of the papier-mâché recipe were shredded paper, flour, glue and ashes. Their hair was usually moulded and their features were naively modelled resembling wooden dolls of the same period. They had wooden limbs attached to a kid body, and spoon-shaped hands with only a separate thumb.

CHINA

These dolls were at their height in the mid-19th century. They have a shiny finish unlike that of bisque dolls. Usually they were mould cast and have shoulder-heads with moulded hair and a kid body. They were mostly produced in Germany, although some were also made in France.

PARIAN

Parian dolls were made from unglazed, untinted, hard-paste porcelain. They have a white flesh tone and matt finish like that of bisque dolls. Parians were chiefly made in Germany during the 19th century and resemble porcelain dolls of the time. They were often moulded with pieces of jewellery which were painted and fired with facial details.

BISQUE

Made from unglazed, tinted porcelain, bisque became popular in both France and Germany from the mid-19th to the 20th century for top-quality fashion dolls, girl dolls, bébés and characters. The head or shoulder-plate was cast in a mould and fired. It was cleaned, sanded and painted to give a skin colour. The facial details were painted on and it was fired again. Hands and feet might also be bisque, but on this late-19th century Gaultier fashion doll they are kid like the rest of the body. Typically, this example has gusseted hips and knees which will enable the doll to sit.

CLOTH

Cloth dolls range from primitive home-made examples to the intricate 19th and early-20th century ones made by Käthe Kruse, Steiff and Lenci. Examples earlier than the late-19th century are extremely rare since fabric dolls usually do not survive.

COMPOSITION

After 1900, some American and German factories made dolls in composition, a substance comprising papier-mâché with added sawdust. Before 1914 the cold-press method of construction was used. This had the disadvantage that the top layer peeled away in time. This fault was rectified by the hot-press method in which heat was applied during the moulding process. Composition dolls usually have a seam running down the side of the head. They are difficult to clean without damaging their varnish and bisque-headed dolls with composition bodies like the Armand Marseille girl or the Bruno Schmidt character baby (below left and right respectively) are more desirable than dolls with head and body both made from composition.

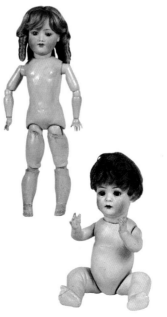

CELLULOID

Celluloid was the term used from 1870 to refer to an inexpensive alternative to bisque developed in the United States. Some celluloid dolls were made in Bavaria, France and Japan. The disadvantage was that the material was easily dented and flammable. They were modelled both as babies and children. The celluloid has a noticeably glossy sheen and also has a lightweight feel compared with hard plastic.

VINYL AND HARD PLASTIC

Hard plastic dolls were made briefly after the Second World War. But by the mid-1950s they had been mostly replaced by vinyl, which is much softer. Plastic dolls had moulded hair or wigs, while vinyl dolls have rooted hair. Both types of doll must be in excellent condition to be valuable, and preferably with the hair as originally set.

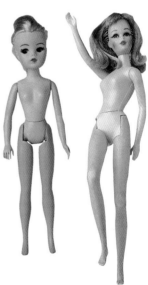

DOLLS: BODIES

The body of a doll is all-important in assessing its origin, history and value. The variation is enormous, especially in the case of bisque. Although the heads are all of the same material, the bodies may not be, and construction style and quality vary hugely. A knowledge of different body types is thus invaluable in identifying a particular doll and in spotting 'wrong' replaced limbs. The examples here are among the bodies most commonly found.

◀ **EARLY WOODEN**
English wooden dolls before 1740 were round-faced with long wide necks. The head and torso were usually in one piece, the waist was tapered, the hands forked and the upper arms possibly cloth.

▶ **FASHION SHAPES**
Bisque shoulder-headed fashion dolls often had gusseted kid bodies with wide hips and shoulders to suit period dress. Forearms were sometimes bisque and tenon joints used at shoulders, elbows and knees.

◀ **LATER WOODEN**
From 1740 wooden dolls had slimmer necks, sloping shoulders and a skittle-shaped torso with a high bust and no waist, although after 1780 the neck thickened again and the features became cruder.

◀ **PAPIER-MÂCHÉ**
The deep-yolked shoulder-heads of pre-1870 German papier-mâché dolls were glued to bodies of kid or calico. They were unjointed, with a narrow waist and wide hips. Some dolls had wooden lower limbs.

▶ **FIRST BÉBÉS**
Early French bébés with a bisque head and jointed body had their limb parts connected by means of a ball which was fixed to one of the limbs.

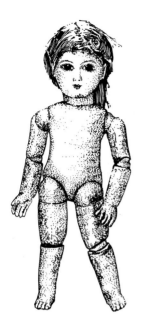

▶ JOINTED TODDLERS
German jointed toddlers had wood or composition bodies with pronounced side-hip joints and fat tummies, as used on character dolls produced after 1910.

▲ BALL JOINTS
Some bisque-head dolls have eight ball-jointed or floating-ball-jointed bodies. In this case the limbs slide over an unattached floating-ball joint.

◀ NE PLUS ULTRA
In 1833 an American patented the ne plus ultra body with a bisque shoulder-head, composition or leather arms and jointed knees and elbows. Unusually, the body forms part of the thigh.

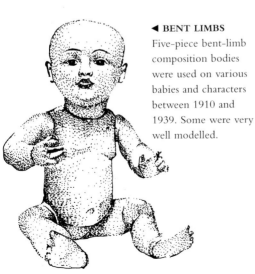

◀ BENT LIMBS
Five-piece bent-limb composition bodies were used on various babies and characters between 1910 and 1939. Some were very well modelled.

▶ FLAPPER LEGS
From 1920 German composition bodies were made with flapper legs. The knee joints were set noticeably higher than on earlier dolls.

DOLLS: HEADS

Dolls are classified according to head type. The style and quality of the head can assist in dating and identifying a doll, while a good knowledge of the 'right' combinations of heads and bodies is vital in authentication. The head is also the most important factor governing the value of a doll and is what you look at first. Since many dolls' heads are hand-painted, examine the attention to detail, the artistry of the expression and also the skill in shading. Hair should be as realistic and eyes as lifelike as possible.

The following examples are among the most common or distinctive heads.

SHOULDER-HEADS

Many early dolls have shoulder-heads. This means that the shoulders, neck and head are moulded in one piece. The shoulder-plate reaches the top of the arms. The head might be glued into a kid body or sewn, using specially made holes, onto a cloth body. This type of head was introduced with the earliest papier-mâché dolls. Shoulder-heads were more versatile and often cheaper than making the head part of a whole torso, as was the case with many wooden dolls.

SWIVEL HEADS

On a swivel-headed doll the head and shoulder-plate are separate. The head fits into a cup on the shoulder-plate, which may be lined with kid, enabling the head to swivel.

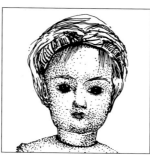

OPEN HEADS

Bisque dolls very often have an open head. The open section is the crown. This is covered with a separate pate (cork on French dolls, cardboard on German) and is the section to which the wig is attached. The pate is stuck to the bisque rim.

SOLID DOMED

The few bisque-headed dolls with solid-domed heads are called Belton heads. They can be socket heads, a later form of swivel head, or shoulder-plate heads. Wigs are stuck with glue. Sometimes the head has holes, with the wig held by string.

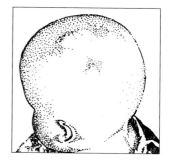

FLANGE NECK

The flange neck is often used on soft-bodied dolls such as Dream Babies. The base of the open neck curves outwards with two holes positioned so that the head can be sewn onto the body.

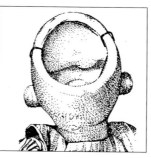

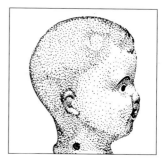

SOCKET HEAD

The most common head type on the majority of French and German dolls and babies is the socket head. The base of the neck is rounded so that the head fits into a cup-shape at the top of the body.

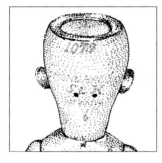

EYES

Painted eyes were used on dolls made from all materials. 'Intaglio' eyes, a development of painted eyes in which the eye is carved out of the head and highlighted with white, are found on many character dolls. Fixed glass eyes, usually dark with no pupil, were used on 18th-century wooden and 19th-century wax and papier-mâché dolls. 'Paperweight' eyes were made from blown glass and the irises appear to have a greater depth due to radiating spirals of colour within the glass. Sleeping or 'sleep eyes', which can open and close, were used on some wax-over-composition/papier-mâché dolls. At first they were operated by a wire lever but by the end of the 19th century they were controlled instead by a weight. 'Flirty' eyes are glass eyes which not only close but also move from side-to-side when the head is tilted. They are found on early 20th-century character dolls. 'Googly' eyes are exaggeratedly round and side-glancing. They have given their name to a type of 20th-century doll.

MOUTHS

The earliest dolls had closed mouths. Open-closed mouths with the lips slightly apart but the paste uncut appear on early bisque dolls made by Bru and on German characters. An open mouth with teeth was first used in about 1900 by both French and German makers. 'Watermelon' or closed smiling mouths drawn as a thin line were part of the charm of Googlies and Kewpies. Today, closed-mouthed dolls are considered more appealing and are more sought after than those with open mouths.

EARS

Some early wooden dolls had carved ears, although many had none. Most French fashion and some better quality German dolls had the added detail of pierced ears and earrings. Ceramic dolls usually had ears moulded with the head and some larger bébés had applied ears.

PATES

'Pate' is the term used for the covering of the head aperture where the wigs were attached. The pate gives a rounded rather than a flat or indented effect. French dolls used cork pates, harvested from Portuguese 'cork oak' trees. German dolls had cardboard pates which were moulded and cut to fit snugly into the aperture and glued with light fish glue. The German firm of Kestner was known for making 'plaster' pates which were difficult to remove.

HAIR

The best early wooden dolls had hair attached to a cloth cap which was nailed to the head. Most other dolls either had painted or moulded and painted hair until the middle of the 19th century when wigs of human hair and mohair became common. Bisque, celluloid and plastic dolls generally had a wig attached to a cardboard or cork pate. The most expensive poured-wax dolls and some fabric dolls had hairs inserted into the wax or sewn in, and vinyl dolls have rooted synthetic hair which is inserted in clumps.

DOLLS: HAIRSTYLES

Hairstyles can be a valuable clue to dating on china and parian dolls, although wigs on other dolls may have been replaced. The more elaborate the hairstyle, the more valuable the doll. Hats, feathers, snoods, jewellery, plaits, colour and lustre, all moulded and fired, add extra worth. Similarly with painted hair: the more decorative or appropriate to the character, the better. Real hair or mohair wigs are of less consequence since they are very frequently damaged by combing and handling. Synthetic rooted hair suffers similarly but good condition matters to the value. In Barbie's case, an original hairstyle is an important bonus.

The hairstyles worn by parian and china dolls reflect the fashions of the second half of the 19th century and are a help with dating dolls. Here are a selection of styles and the approximate years when they were popular.

1850

1850

1850

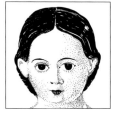

1860

1865

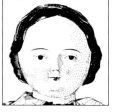

1865

1865

1865

1870

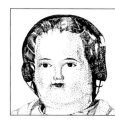

1870

1870

1870   1870   1870   1870

1870

1870

1870

1870

1870

1875

1875

1880

1880

1880

1880

1880

1880

1880

1880

1880

1885

1885

1885

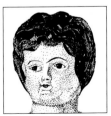

1890

TEDDY BEARS: MATERIALS, SHAPE & CONSTRUCTION

Clues to a bear's age, make and authenticity lie in its fabric, shape and how it has been made. Is it mohair plush or synthetic fibre? How long are its limbs – is the bear gangly or chubby? Is it naturalistic or stylized in design?

How long is its snout? How big are its ears? What are its eyes made of, and its nose?

Since many were never marked or else have long since lost their labels, it is worthwhile remembering the following pointers.

EYES

The first German bears had black button eyes made from metal or wood, generally stitched to the head or attached by wires or hooks. These are referred to as boot-button eyes. Shortly before the First World War glass eyes attached by wire shanks became common, although other types also turn up including moving googly eyes, enamelled metal eyes and painted clear-glass eyes. The eyes of black Steiff bears were set against circles of red felt. Earlier bears tended to have eyes set closer together than later ones. From 1955 onwards plastic eyes were used because they were safer for children. Later plastic eyes tend to be larger, as were glass eyes. Safety standards which have been introduced since the use of plastic became widespread require plastic eyes to be firmly fixed.

EARS

The position of the ears and their size and shape can typify a certain make. Merrythought usually had widely spaced ears, most notably in this Cheeky bear introduced in 1957. Besides being excessively large, the ears have a bell stitched inside them. From 1927–30, Steiff made bears which had wired ears that could be moved into different positions. Known as Petsys, they are much sought after.

SEAMS

Body seams are usually placed down the middle. Steiff bears, however, sometimes have a seam running down the front of the face marking where one bolt of cloth ran out and the next was started. Ironically, this makes these bears especially valuable.

SNOUTS & NOSES

This bear's profile shows the realistic appearance of early Steiffs. Long, clipped snouts gradually gave way to a stubbier, often hairier, versions. Early noses were of sealing wax or hand-embroidered, the shape and direction of the stitching varying according to the maker. Rubber noses were introduced after 1950 and many modern bears have plastic noses.

STUFFING

Early German bears were stuffed with 'excelsior', which is wood shavings used for packing. Other bears, especially English and German bears of the 1920s, were sometimes stuffed with kapok, a soft silky fibre from certain seed pods, while some teddies were filled with a mixture. Post-war bears frequently have a synthetic, machine-washable stuffing lighter than shavings or kapok.

PAWS

Felt was the most usual material for early bears, as in this Steiff example. The most popular colours were beige, brown and cream although black bears might have black paws. The felt was often reinforced with fabric or cardboard under the pad. Leather paws have been used throughout the 20th century. Cotton, velveteen and woven cotton was popular between 1930 and 1950. Wrexine, a type of oil cloth, was used from 1930 to the 1950s. Synthetic plush paws came in after 1950.

LIMBS

Long limbs were the norm among early bears, quite astonishingly so in the case of the Steiff bear below. However, both shrank at a varying rate according to make, arms and legs. This was partly a matter of fashion but partly as a result of post-war shortages. Long-limbed bears are usually more valuable because they are probably by Steiff and earlier.

FABRICS

Prior to 1945, most bears were of silk mohair plush, made from the wool of the angora goat. Dual-coloured mohair plush which had dark tips and a pale base was fashionable in the 1920s. Synthetic fibres became common after the Second World War and are much shinier and harder to the touch. Makers also began to experiment with harsher, more unrealistic colours. Not surprisingly, natural fibres are more desirable.

BODIES

Over the years, the shape of bears became more barrel-like as in the Deans bear c.1950 below. Originally they were modelled on real bears, but makers competed to produce a new look. The change is most noticeable after the Second World War. Being earlier, the longer, more ungainly type is liable to be worth more – especially if it happens to be a Steiff with a hump at the top of its back.

JOINTS

Most bears are disc-jointed at the hips, shoulders and neck, the discs made of cardboard and held in place with a metal pin. Metal-rod Steiff bears, identifiable only by x-ray for sure, are the most sought after.

MARKS

The Steiff invention of a button in the ear was copied as a method of labelling by various firms, including Merrythought and Chad Valley. Because of the Steiff patent, Bing placed their button under the arm. Unfortunately, anxious parents often removed such buttons as they were potentially dangerous. Fabric labels were often stitched to a foot or inserted in a seam, but these may have been lost if the paws have been replaced. Paper labels were frequently attached to a bear's chest but these have rarely survived.

TEDDY BEARS & DOLLS:
FAKES, MARRIAGES & ALTERATIONS

Certain types or makes of bear and doll are now so valuable that it is well worth a faker's effort to forge an early Steiff or an exquisite French bébé from scratch. Alternatively, unscrupulous dealers often 'improve' on lesser items. Both play upon a collector's desire to secure a 'find' or a bargain and the all-too-human tendency to believe something is right just because you want it to be. So it is very important always to be on your guard.

FAKES

Probably the most troubling fakes on the market are supposed early Steiff bears. They have what look like genuine Steiff buttons, are thought to be made in England and usually turn up in small country auctions or are slipped into car boot sales, where sufficient comparison with other genuine Steiff bears is unlikely. The same happens with 'aged' wooden dolls which were supposedly found in a wealthy deceased relative's attic.

REPRODUCTIONS

Bear artists are sometimes inclined to reproduce old bears for fun. Unfortunately, after they have changed hands a few times eager owners may get carried away with their claims. So try to establish a bear's provenance and beware if a teddy is looking too pristine. Reproduction dolls are also usually made for fun by enthusiasts, but Britain's most famous forger Tom Keating said his fake paintings were a joke. The trouble arises later, as with 'Barbies' which were made as copies in the Far East.

CLUES TO WATCH

A good clue to a fake is that the wear patches are in the wrong places, such as under the arms or inside the legs – as in the top bear to the left. Note also if there are extra-long hind pads, shapeless arms and odd jointing of any kind.

It is very difficult to stitch the head or snout of a bear and this is therefore a key area to observe. An incorrect shape and mis-stitching would be a good indication of a bear that is not genuine. The jointing at the shoulders and hips is also a tell-tale place and over-stuffing with straw gives a rigid effect – as in the bottom bear.

REPLICAS

Old bears were becoming so popular in the 1980s that Steiff began to make limited-edition replicas of some of the firm's early stock. Other manufacturers quickly followed suit. These teddies are being made in the traditional way and could be confusing. So be aware of these new collectables, even if only to avoid them. Limited editions of other early soft toys are also on the market and a favourite unscrupulous trick is to mix authentically old animals and replicas, especially in Noah's Ark sets. Replica bébés and other especially desirable dolls are also being produced in limited editions.

MARRIAGES

After examining the parts of a doll, look at it as a whole to make sure the body is correct for the head. Sometimes when a doll has been damaged, the head is rescued and 'married' to another doll's body. Check that joints fit comfortably into their sockets, especially the head and neck. Watch out also for replaced limbs. Do not buy a doll without undressing it first.

The bisque-headed doll with a papier-mâché body (opposite, above left) may appear fine clothed. When undressed, however, it becomes obvious that the head, which is a Simon & Halbig, is too large for the body, which is a Steiner. One owner of the Simon & Halbig bisque-headed doll (bottom left) has tried to get away with too cheap a replacement kid body. Not only is it too small but the hands are composition when they should be bisque since the head is identifiable as No. 941 of earlier child-faced moulds.

Teddy bears are less prone to inconvenient marriages, but anything is possible. It is simply more difficult to match up a bear's head and body, even when both are made of the same material. It is more likely that a single limb or pair of limbs have been replaced on one bear from a similar, deceased teddy. Ears are even more difficult. Replicas make the faker's job easier, as all the visible materials used on them are traditional. Probably the biggest problem is the marriage of the wrong bear with a value-enhancing story. If anyone tries to sell you the bear owned by Christopher Robin that inspired A.A. Milne, or the original Paddington who came from Selfridge's, not Peru, just say 'no'. Even museums have been fooled by documentation that is all too easy to forge.

ALTERATIONS

If the 1780s wooden doll (below centre) were in perfect condition with its original clothes it would be worth four times as much. However, someone has replaced the original wooden arms in cloth and given the doll new legs. The head has not been restored, so without close inspection the doll may appear completely original. New paw pads are the most usual repair to a bear.

RIGHT OR WRONG

A trick that may be used by dealers is to claim that something is 'unique'. How can you check if something is 'right' or 'wrong' when there is nothing with which to compare it? The supposedly 19th-century wooden doll shown below, suggested as north Italian, is an example. It is well carved and had the advantage of being in the renowned Bodmer Collection. It sold at Sotheby's for twice as much as expected and nothing similar could be located. The doll still remains a puzzle today.

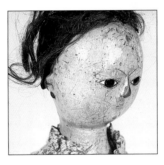

PART 4

TEDDY BEAR FILE

ABOVE TWO EARLY J.K. FARNELL TEDDY BEARS
MADE IN BRITAIN 1918. £800–1,200

LEFT TWO STEIFF TEDDY BEARS, ONE CINNAMON
PLUSH AND THE OTHER SILVER PLUSH, BOTH
GERMAN, C.1908. £5,000–7,000 EACH

Opinion is divided concerning the first teddy-bear creator. Margarete Steiff of Giengen, south Germany, studied dressmaking and in 1877 opened a clothes shop. Although confined to a wheelchair by polio since childhood, she created some tiny felt elephant-shaped pincushions as family presents and went on to make different animal toys, including the first bear standing on all fours in 1884, which she sold at local fairs. She set up business with her nephew Richard, who devised the first jointed bear. Exhibited at the 1903 Leipzig Toy Fair it attracted a large US order. Steiff claimed that when President 'Teddy' Roosevelt was unable to name the bears' breed they were dubbed 'Teddy's bears'.

Inventor Morris Michtom, a Russian immigrant in New York noted President Roosevelt's refusal to shoot a cub on a Mississippi bear hunt. A Clifford Berryman cartoon of the scene in the *Washington Post*, *Drawing the Line at Mississippi*, referred to the President's fair-mindedness and his attempt to settle a Mississippi/Alabama border dispute. Michtom's wife made a soft, jointed bear and displayed it in her sweet-shop window, Michtom having sought the President's permission to call it 'Teddy'. A bear became Roosevelt's campaign mascot.

An apocryphal British version has a pyjama salesman calling at Buckingham Palace to sell his wares to Edward VII. The Queen is supposed to have muttered, "We much prefer our Teddy bare".

The earliest Steiff bears and those by Ideal, the company founded by Michtom, can be worth many thousands of pounds.

STEIFF I

In 1903, Steiff sold 12,000 teddy bears. The following year Margarete Steiff registered the elephant trademark which was to be attached to all Steiff products. The bears were relatively realistic as her nephew and designer, Richard Steiff, modelled them on living animals.

▲ **CONDITION**
Although the excellent condition of this bear, nicknamed Chester, adds to its value, it sadly indicates that it has never been played with and truly enjoyed by children. Note also the tiny bear peeking out from Chester's pocket. These miniature Steiff bears are very desirable and are often worth as much as larger ones. Both bears were made in 1907 and carry the later Steiff trademark in their ear. They are especially valuable because of their rare colour and mint state.
£12,000–14,000

WHAT TO LOOK FOR
● The Steiff trademark. Originally there was an elephant logo on a button in the ear. This was replaced in 1905–6 by a button bearing the firm's name.
● Most pre-First World War bears have black boot- or shoe-button eyes, while later examples have glass eyes.
● A naturalistic style: pre-1940 bears are distinguished by long, curved arms and legs and spoon-shaped front paws.

ROD BEAR

A VERY RARE 1904
ROD TEDDY BEAR.
ALTHOUGH BEARS OF
THIS TYPE ARE
GENERALLY OF HIGH
VALUE, THE VALUE OF
THIS ONE IS LOWER
BECAUSE THE PLUSH
FUR IS WORN ALL
OVER AND THERE IS A
HOLE IN THE TUMMY.
£12,000–15,000

There is a distinctive
hump at the top of the
back.

The ankles are narrow
and the feet are large
and oval.

The ears are widely
positioned and
slightly clipped.

The traditional boot-
button eyes are placed
low and close to the
muzzle, which is
prominent and pointed.

This elephant-shaped
button in the ear is the
trademark of the early
Steiff bears.

The sealing-wax nose is
unique to early rod-
jointed bears.

The arms on this are
unusually long, even for
a Steiff bear.

The coat is made of
golden plush.

◀ NOVELTY BEARS
Steiff made many
novelty bears. This
blonde plush muzzled
bear was produced in
1908 and has
many of the
characteristic
features of early
bears, including a
growler in its stomach,
first introduced that
year. Muzzled bears
were probably inspired
by the traditional
German dancing
bears, which
travelled from town
to town with their
trainers. However,
they were never
popular with children
and the line was
discontinued after
several years. Their
rarity adds much
to their value.
£12,000–14,000

▲ TOO MUCH LOVE
Excessive carrying
around for comfort or
luck has greatly
lowered the value of
this 1918 Steiff bear.
£150–200

STEIFF II

▶ ALFONZO

Alfonzo is among the rarest coloured teddy bears produced by Steiff and has an illustrious history. This red bear was given in 1908 to the Russian Princess Xenia Georgievna, great-great granddaughter of Catherine the Great, by her father George Michailovich, the Grand Duke of Russia. The Duke was assassinated in the Russian Revolution, but Princess Xenia was in England at the time. In 1921 she married William Leeds, heir to a tin fortune, and moved to America. Alfonzo went with her and she died there in 1965. By 1989 Alfonzo was back in England for auction at Christie's South Kensington, where Ian Pout, the owner of Teddy Bears of Witney, bought him. £20,000–25,000

▶ ROLY-POLY BEARS

Roly-Poly bears were made between 1909 and 1914 to entertain babies by rolling to and fro when knocked. The bear is permanently fixed to a curved wooden base. This example is very play-worn and is worth only £500–600: a similar example in good condition would be worth £800–1,200.

STUFFING

The first Steiff bears were filled with excelsior, a mixture of fine, long wood shavings sometimes mistakenly called straw stuffing. The shavings' thickness increased over the years, giving the bears a firmer feel. Kapok, a cotton-like or silky fibre from the seeds of the tropical kapok tree, was used later, sometimes together with excelsior around the voice boxes of early bears.

◀ BLACK BEARS

This is one of only 494 Steiff black teddy bears, which were made in 1912 for the British market. Red felt discs had to be inserted behind the boot-button eyes to throw them into relief. Babies and children were so frightened of these bears that they were never made again. Especially valuable because of its condition. £20,000–25,000

GROWLERS

Voice boxes with papered bellows were introduced in 1905. In 1908 these were replaced with automatic ones and in 1912 voice boxes were inserted. Growling ability does not necessarily add to a bear's value, since they were common. Very few voice boxes work today, This is mainly a result of excessive use and shaking of the bear to make him 'talk', which causes the paper attached to the bellows to wear out and develop holes.

▲ **SOMERSAULTING BEARS**
Novelty features of some Steiff bears include the ability to somersault. Both arms are wound forward, as if winding a clockwork toy, and this provides the momentum for a somersault.
£1,500–1,800

▲ **NOSES**
Brown stitched noses are characteristic of white, blond, or silver plush bears; black noses of brown or gold bears. Until the end of the 1920s a small piece of felt was inserted beneath the nose stitching to give a realistic contour. Stitches are generally vertical on larger bears, but may be horizontal on smaller ones. This 27 in (69 cm) 1905 silver bear has its original price tag and is in mint condition.
£10,000–15,000

◀ **AGEING**
Cinnamon-coloured bears are prone to ageing because of the dye used. Many Steiff bears have new pads because the felt used was fragile. These do not reduce the value of a bear if correctly replaced, but missing ears or fur are irreplaceable. Bears such as this 1908 example were made from 12 in (30 cm) to 28 in (67 cm) tall and are worth between £3,000 and £10,000.

BEWARE

The high prices that Steiff bears can now command have resulted in an increasing number of fakes. Some have fake buttons in the ear. Others, and these are more misleading, have genuine buttons taken from less expensive Steiff dolls or worn-out bears.

OTHER EUROPEAN TEDDY BEARS

Many German firms were quick to jump on the teddy bandwagon in the early 1900s. Their bears were frequently unmarked, which can make them difficult to identify. Among the most notable makers were Hermann (whose bears were similar to Steiff bears), Schuco and Bing, some of whose mechanical novelties, such as the somersaulting bear, are especially highly prized. Examples are generally rare since production was disrupted by the advent of the First World War. In Britain the First World War actually boosted the teddy bear industry. Imports from Germany were banned and companies such as Dean's Rag Book Company Ltd (which had started making bears in 1905), Farnell and Chiltern soon stepped in to fill the gap. The French bear industry was also boosted by the absence of German imports during the First World War, although it remained very much a home market. Most early bears were rod jointed and often had a metal button in the ear, which was in imitation of Steiff bears. The leading manufacturer was M. Pintel Fils & Cie.

MAJOR GERMAN MAKERS

HERMANN – This company was started in 1907 by Johann Hermann near Sonneberg and continued by his son Bernhard, who established his own business nearby in 1911. Sonneberg was then the world centre of toymaking and the place where many important American purchasers, such as Woolworth, had offices for buying bears to import to North America. Hermann bears are completely jointed like Steiff and made of the best quality mohair plush. However, their features are a little less accentuated than the Steiff design – the muzzle possibly shorter and maybe of a different material from the rest of the bear. Bears produced until 1929 also have identity tags with the letters 'BEHA'. Hermann bears are much sought after by collectors. £800–1,000

SCHUCO – Noted for mechanical bears and miniatures, Schuco was established in 1912 by the teenage Heinrich Muller and a partner called Schreyer. The name is an abbreviation of Schreyer und Co. Production ceased when Muller and Schreyer were drafted to fight in the First World War. Schreyer left after the war, but Muller kept the name and restarted production with a new partner. Small facial features and feet are characteristic of early Schuco bears. £1,500–2,000

▲ **J.K. FARNELL**
The famous English doll and toy firm, founded in the mid-nineteenth century by Agnes Farnell, claims to have invented the teddy bear as the firm produced rabbit-skin animal toys from at least 1897 and then distributed them in Germany and also elsewhere. These two bears £800–1200 and £1000–1500.

▶ **CHILTERN**
Bavarian-born Leon Rees, dollmaker since 1912, owned Chiltern Toy Works, Chesham, Buckinghamshire. One of his first teddy bears was a Master Teddy which featured as a *Daily Mail* character in *The Teddy Tail League*. £2,000–3,000

THE HAY BEAR

THIS BEAR, BELIEVED TO HAVE BEEN MADE BY FARNELL IN 1915, IS DRESSED IN THE UNIFORM OF THE GORDON HIGHLANDERS, IN HAY TARTAN AND CONTEMPORARY UNIFORM. THE BEAR BELONGED TO THE SON OF CAPTAIN HAY WHO WAS AWAY FIGHTING IN THE FIRST WORLD WAR. THE UNIFORM WAS MADE BY THE BOY'S NANNY. THE PIPS ON THE UNIFORM MEAN THE BEAR MUST BE PRE-1916. £3,000–4,000

The plush is top-quality mohair, also called Yorkshire cloth.

The snout is prominent and clipped.

The arms are long and curved.

Farnell ears are often situated high on the head.

The eyes are large and made of amber-and-black glass.

The nose is vertically stitched.

The paw-pads are made of cotton twill or felt.

◀ BING

Gebrüder Bing, the Bing brothers of Nüremberg, began making tin kitchenware in 1865 and then enamelled toys in 1890. They added teddy bears to their output before the First World War. Bing bears are often dressed in colourful outfits made of felt and silk. As with Schuco bears they are noted for their mechanical abilities, such as walking, and their small facial features. In some instances they have an identity tag fixed to the ear. Before 1919, these tags bore the letters G.B.N. (Gebrüder Bing, Nuremberg), afterwards, B.W. (Bing Werke). This clockwork, football-playing bear believed to have been made by Bing in 1910 is less valuable than it might be because of its small size. £600–800

NORTH AMERICAN TEDDY BEARS

Morris Michtom (see page 48) set up the Ideal Novelty & Toy Company and sales escalated. Unfortunately its bears were never labelled. Other important makers included the Knickerbocker Toy Co (see page 62), whose bears have a label in a front centre seam saying: "Knickerbocker Toy Co. New York". The Fast Black Skirt Company produced bears whose novelty features included squeaking, growling, whistling, laughing, tumbling (the most desirable) and musical effects.

Battery-operated eyes are activated by pressing a button in the bear's stomach.

Some bears were made with two faces: a teddy-bear face and a doll's. Another variation was a bear's body with a doll's head, known as a Teddy Doll and produced by Hahn and Amberg in New York in 1908, followed in 1909 by E.I. Horsman's extraordinary Billiken dolls with teddy-bear bodies and grotesque elfin features. These were an instant success but are now less valuable than Teddy Dolls.

CHARACTERISTICS OF A 1907 IDEAL TEDDY BEAR. £2,000–2,500

The ears are large, rounded and widely placed.

The eyes are made of glass or shoe buttons (the latter are earlier) and are usually attached by wires to the side seams of the face.

The head is triangular.

The snout is prominently pointed with a D-shaped nose made of twill and a stitched mouth.

The fur around the muzzle is often shorn on earlier bears.

The bear has a swivel neck.

The paw pads are made of felt and often pointed at the tip.

This bear is jointed at the hips and shoulders, as are all Ideal bears.

The fur is mohair plush and still in good condition.

◀▶ LAUGHING ROOSEVELT
Made in 1908 by Columbia
Teddy Bears in New York, this
bear is jointed with the addition
of two rows of white glass teeth,
giving him a very lifelike
appearance. Squeezing a
mechanism in the stomach
causes the mouth to open and
close in a fearsome manner.
The eyes are made of black
buttons. £2,000–3,000

▼ BOOTS
Boots belonged to Colonel Bob
Henderson who served under
General Montgomery and
founded the Good Bears of the
World Society to help sick
children. Boots was given to
Henderson by an old lady with
a note saying : "Please look after
my bear". £4,000–5,000

**▶ FOOTBALL-SHAPED
BEARS**
Unmarked, early Ideal bears
can often be identified by their
generously proportioned, barrel-
shaped bodies, often with a
small, pointed hump at the back
of the neck. They are much
wider than German bears of the
same date and referred to by
American collectors as 'football-
shaped'. In this example, the
pads have been replaced.
£1,600–1,800

◀ FASHION
Most early Ideal bears were
produced in short gold or beige
mohair plush with matching
felt paws. Later bears were more
varied and often had longer fur.
This 1910 mohair bear is
29 in (76 cm) tall and also has
an original sailor suit. Ideal
made complete wardrobes for
bears but were not very prolific
in comparison with Steiff.
  Many of the clothes would
have been produced by a
variety of other companies.
£300–500

BEWARE
Because early Ideal bears
are so desirable, fakes are
being produced. Be
suspicious of bears with
no sign of wear or
restoration and bears with
uneven seams or thickly
stitched, unworn noses.

By the end of the First World War, increasing numbers of doll and toy manufacturers were bringing out their own teddy bears since this popular new toy was fairly easy to produce, as long as the aspiring manufacturer had a talented seamstress, a pattern and a sewing machine. Steiff's biggest rivals in Germany remained Hermann, Schuco and Bing.

Ideal went from strength to strength in America along with a growing number of other manufacturers and the passion caught on worldwide. In England, Farnell and Dean's Rag Book Co (who had come into their own thanks to the First World War) were joined by many more. Farnell are probably the most desirable early English bears, although Dean's, Chad Valley, Merrythought and Chiltern are also very collectable. English bears are often softer than German ones because British makers tended to prefer kapok stuffing to excelsior, which was usually used in Germany.

The Second World War severely disrupted the European teddy bear industry. After the war ended, manufacturers began to use synthetic fibres much more. Bears with synthetic coats are generally less valuable. The increasing collectability of old bears has led to the artificial 'ageing' of traditional, new bears and the adding of spurious labels or buttons to genuinely old bears of unknown make which may, for example, resemble Steiff. Since many genuine old bears are unmarked, novice collectors need to be especially careful. Prices depend on the age, colour, condition, rarity and, most of all, the maker.

GERMAN TEDDY BEARS

Steiff, noted for their attention to detail and their bears' durability, was emulated by other German manufacturers but continued to lead the market. Body shapes, however, began to change and features became less exaggerated. The hump almost disappeared, the nose became shorter, the arms lost their deep curve and the feet grew smaller.

▲ **TEDDY CLOWN**
This Teddy Clown, with hat and ruff, has distinctively large glass eyes set close together and is soft to cuddle because it is stuffed with kapok instead of excelsior. It was patented by Steiff in North America in 1926. The Teddy Clown was made in pink, gold or brown-tipped mohair plush and sold in 11 different sizes, from 9 in (23 cm) to 45 in (114 cm) tall. These clowns were so popular that 30,000 were manufactured in 1928, of which this is one.
£5,000–8,000

◀ TEDDY BABY
Steiff Teddy Babies, modelled on a real cub, were produced from 1929 to the 1950s. The bear's extra-large, cardboard-reinforced flat feet allowed it to stand. Examples which are pre-Second World War are the most sought after. This 1948 bear, however, at 64in (163cm)

tall is possibly the world's largest jointed Steiff bear. Made for a German department store, it has the same characteristics as smaller versions: an open, pale orange felt mouth, black stitched nose, large black-and-brown glass eyes, a swivel neck and downward-facing paws with stitched claws. £4,000–6,000

◀ MINIATURES
A 1920s black and white miniature is rarer than the golden 1930s miniature, while the 1938 pink Schuco miniature in a three-wheeler is worth the most. This is because unusual colours such as pink, purple and green command much higher prices, provided the bears are in excellent condition. £500–800

▼ HERMANN
Bernhard Hermann's three sons followed in his footsteps and the firm was relocated in 1948 to Hirschaid near Bamberg, where the name became Gebrüder Hermann. The identity tag 'BEHA' was changed in 1930 to 'Marke BEHA Teddy', then

from 1940–51 to 'Hermann Teddy' ('Teddy' is always underlined). This 1920s 'Zotty' type (named after a German storybook character), with its original ribbon and bell, is in good condition but is not as collectable as the more usual-looking bears. £300–400

▶ PETSY BEARS
Made only from 1927–30, Petsy Bears' distinctive features give it rather a comical appearance. The name stems from a storybook bear called Petz. Petsies are soft like Teddy Clowns as they are filled with kapok, and are made in two-tone mohair – in this case blond with brown tips. Unmistakably, however, they also have

moveable googly eyes made of blue glass, wired ears (which can be placed in different positions), a seam running down the centre of the face and a red stitched nose – which will probably have faded to pink. £3,500–5,000

BRITISH TEDDY BEARS I

British teddy-bear manufacture took off after the First World War while German firms were still in disarray. Various features such as the Steiff identity button were imitated but bears tended to be stubbier in shape. The top names were Farnell, Dean's, Chiltern, Chad Valley and Merrythought, although numerous firms were established to meet increasing demand and some endeavoured to keep production going through the Second World War: bears joined the Burma Campaign and were even parachuted into Arnhem.

Hugmee bears were very popular during this period. They have a sorrowful look with head and nose angled downwards. The ears are small and sit oddly far up on the head.

WHAT TO LOOK FOR

● Chiltern Toys were renowned for their soft mohair plush, which had a long pile and was of the finest quality. In top condition this can greatly increase the bear's value.
● Look also for the shaved muzzle, amber and black eyes, stitched nose with upward stitching at either end, long, curving arms and wide feet with velvet pads which are reinforced with cardboard.

◀ CHILTERN TOYS
In 1920 H.G. Stone teamed up with Leon Rees as H.G. Stone & Co. In 1924 the company was registered as Chiltern Toys, after the name of the Buckinghamshire factory where the bears were produced. Noted for the rare 1922 Baby Teddy, Chiltern Toys was quickly established as a leading manufacturer. This 16 in- (41 cm-) tall Winter Skater from the 1930s has felt pads and arms wired to make them stand away from the body. £500–600

◀ HOME GUARD
As a result of the Second World War, teddy-bear factories ceased most production from 1939–45. Firms were expected to produce wartime necessities such as helmet linings instead. Among the few teddies which were produced is this Chiltern bear dressed as a Home Guard Sergeant. Made in 1940 it has a velvet mohair coat and is non-jointed, making it cheaper to produce than a jointed version. £300–400

MARKS

Chiltern bears have a label on the foot or in a side seam that reads: "Chiltern Hygienic Toys made in England".

▶ ALPHA BEARS

In 1930 Farnell introduced the Alpha range, one of their most popular, and this time placed a label on the foot saying "Farnell's Alpha Toys made in England". Although bombed in 1940, production continued. Alpha bears have large feet and rather short legs. The early ones were made using long mohair plush; later ones, such as this silver plush bear (right) dating from the end of the Second World War, were made using a synthetic fibre and jointed. £300–400

◀ DEAN'S RAG BOOK COMPANY

These bears may be labelled on the foot or have a silver button fixed like Steiff bears. As well as their Evripose bears, Dean's was noted for bears of unusual colours and for novelties such as bears on wheels, for which the advertisement stated "It follows like a well trained pet – all you have to do is pull the string". The magenta mohair bear with velvet pads and blue glass eyes pictured is unlabelled but it may have been made by Dean's in 1928. The head is more angular and the ears more rounded compared with some later editions. £600–800

▶ BERTIE

Bertie, represents the archetypal English bear. Labelled on the foot and made by Dean's in 1938, he is jointed, shaggy and yellow – and stuffed with kapok. Note the unrealistic shape. These were among the less expensive bears, as Samuel Dean thought every child should have one. These are fairly common. £300–400

WHAT TO LOOK FOR

● Dean's trademark showed two dogs fiercely tugging at either side of one of the company's books – the tussle supposedly attesting to the durability of their products.

● After the 1930s, legal requirements asking for more information to be provided on labels meant that the picture had to be dropped to make room.

BRITISH TEDDY BEARS II

◀ CHAD VALLEY
Chad Valley produced teddy bears from the 1920s. Most early bears had golden mohair plush. Bodies were large (sometimes with a hump) with limbs short and fat. Feet, sometimes covered in felt, were small and snouts were defined with horizontally stitched noses. Eyes were of amber-and-black glass attached by wires. Kapok and excelsior were used to create soft limbs and a harder head, as in this 26 in (66 cm) 1930 bear. £650–800

▶ PEACOCK & SONS
Founded in 1853, Peacock were making bears when the firm was taken over by Chad Valley in 1930. This 28-in (71-cm) tall teddy dates from around that time but still has the red-and-white Peacock label on its right foot as the Clerkenwell factory continued under its own name. Note the angular head, chunky arms and the arched and square snout with heavy black stitching, £1400–£1600

MARKS
Early bears were labelled on the foot as shown right: "Hygienic toys, made in England by the Chad Valley Co., Ltd". The label was printed or embroidered in black or red. Metal identity buttons were also used, and labels stitched into side seams. From 1938 to 1953, a square label with a royal crest was stitched to the foot confirming Chad Valley was "Toy Makers to H.M. the Queen" (meaning the wife of King George VI).

WHAT TO LOOK FOR
● The Chad Valley Celluloid button was usually inserted into the right ear.
● Other British makers used textile labels which were sewn either onto the left or right foot.
● Some makers occasionally made use of a label which was sewn in at the side under the arm, round the neck on a collar or as a chest badge.

MERRYTHOUGHT

MERRYTHOUGHT LTD WAS ESTABLISHED NEAR IRONBRIDGE IN SHROPSHIRE IN 1930 BY W.G. HOLMES AND G.H. LAXTON TOGETHER WITH A NUMBER OF EX-EMPLOYEES OF CHAD VALLEY. THE BEARS ARE EASILY CONFUSED WITH CHAD VALLEY BEARS BECAUSE THE CHIEF DESIGNER UNTIL 1949 WAS FLORENCE ATWOOD, THE DEAF-MUTE DAUGHTER OF ONE OF CHAD'S FOUNDERS WHO HAD GAINED EXPERIENCE WORKING WITH NORAH WELLINGS AT CHAD BEFORE SHE TOO LEFT TO SET UP HER OWN BUSINESS. THE NAME MERRYTHOUGHT MEANS 'FORKED BONE' OR 'WISHBONE', AND A WISHBONE WAS ADOPTED AS THE COMPANY TRADEMARK. MERRYTHOUGHT MADE TRADITIONAL BEARS AND NOVELTIES SUCH AS A SITTING BEAR CUB. THIS MERRYTHOUGHT BEAR WAS MADE IN 1930. £600–800

The ears are large, flat and rounded and widely placed across the seams of the head. A celluloid button in the ear, later placed on the back, was used to avoid confusion with Steiff bears.

The arms are long and curving.

The bear is made of good-quality pale-beige, long mohair plush placed over kapok and excelsior stuffing.

The eyes are bulbous and made from amber-and-black glass. They are placed low, emphasizing the prominent forehead.

The nose is vertically stitched with black thread, creating a rectangular shape on the end of a clipped, sharply pointed muzzle.

The paw pads are made of felt. Four claws are indicated by stitching with a connecting stitch across the base.

There is a fabric label attached to the foot.

▶ **WARTIME**
Production of toys, dolls and teddy bears officially stopped in 1941 because of the war effort, so a number of home-made versions from these years may be found today. These are chiefly of curiosity value only, such as the 'nightdress bear' pictured, which was created out of a dress and camel-hair coat. The other was also made out of a camel-hair coat. £40–60

NORTH AMERICAN & OTHER TEDDY BEARS

Fears among manufacturers in North America that teddy-bear popularity would be short-lived proved unfounded. By 1920, Ideal and other firms were still growing as teddies caught on worldwide. An early survey suggested that it was because almost as many bears were bought for adults as for children.

Features often associated with American bears are long, narrow bodies, straightish arms, small feet and short, bristle-type mohair. But the shapes changed and became more stylized as rival firms vied for attention. American firms were notoriously bad at labelling their bears, so identification is often a matter of opinion.

◀ IDEAL
Teddy bears were being produced in a much wider variety of colours. This panda made by Ideal in black-and-white mohair plush with a black stitched nose, black felt paws and a black felt tongue was a popular new range in the 1930s. £300–400

WHAT TO LOOK FOR
● Ideal bears tend to have a triangular-shaped head with small, wide-set eyes.
● Large ears are set on the side of the head.
● The later the bear, the longer the mohair tends to be.

OTHER MAKERS
GUND MANUFACTURING CO – This company was founded in Norwalk, Connecticut by a German emigré called Adolph Gund in 1898, but it did not produce teddy bears until the mid-1920s when the firm had moved to New York. Gund Manufacturing had also been taken over by a partner called Jacob Swedlin, whose descendant still owns the firm. The first bears produced by Gund were made with silk plush. They can be worth £150.
AUSTRALIAN BEARS – The earliest Australian teddy bears were home-made from sheepskin. Australian bear manufacturing was led by Joy-Toys, founded in the 1920s, who also acquired the franchise to produce Walt Disney characters in the 1930s. Look for sheepskin fur with leather pads. £100–150

▲ KNICKERBOCKER
This black mohair plush teddy bear dates from 1920. It is 18 in (46 cm) tall and has typical amber-and-black glass eyes, a gold embroidered nose and mouth and small ears. It is fully jointed, stuffed with excelsior and has velvet paw pads. The features which identify it as Knickerbocker are the particularly heavy triangular head, the large rounded ears and snout and the long torso. £300–500

▶ **CHARACTER TOY CO**
The Character Toy Company was a major producer of teddy bears in Connecticut. The company copied the Steiff idea of putting identification in the ear, although it used a label instead of a button. This 1930s bear with felt pads has the remnants of a label and shows the transition from the long, narrow body to a shorter, rounded style, with larger feet and paws, heavier limbs and no hump. £200–250

BEWARE
Be suspicious of teddy bears which show no obvious sign of wear or restoration: American fakes are increasing.

◀ **BRUTUS THE MYSTERY BEAR**
As so many companies across the United States were producing unlabelled bears, certain identification can prove impossible. This bear, named Brutus, is made of amethyst-coloured mohair plush and was produced in the 1930s. The bear has no label but unusual square shoulders and upturned paws, glass eyes and velvet pads. £400–500

▲ **CHANGING SHAPE**
This bear was made by the Character Toy Company in the 1940s, by which time bears were bcoming even more unrealistic – with cheeky expressions and stylized limbs. They were still usually made fully jointed, in this case from blond mohair plush stuffed with excelsior. It has large, cupped ears, a pointed snout, glass eyes and felt pads. £250–300

▶ **JAPANESE BEARS**
Japanese manufacturers are best known for their post-war, less-expensive and novelty bears which were exported to Europe and the United States. This bear is a 1930s example, jauntily dressed but made from dark brown blanket wool instead of mohair plush. Instead of invisible disc joints, which were used to make good-quality bears, this one has external stapled joints which were much cheaper to produce. Such short-cuts in production immediately reduce a bear's value. Note also the Japanese-style flattened head. £40–60

The production of teddy bears has continued to proliferate and diversify at both the expensive and cheaper ends of the market. Moulded vinyl muzzles first appeared on teddy bears in the early 1950s and rubber or plastic became used for noses later on.

Modern safety standards and alterations in materials available have also led to a number of changes in manufacturing. Eyes, which could be a danger if pulled out and swallowed by small children, are more securely fixed. By the late 1960s, all teddy bears were made with locked in plastic eyes. Stuffing is now often made with man-made fibres. Foam rubber stuffing was tried in the 1950s but later found to emit potentially toxic fumes.

A major introduction has been the production of replica bears in limited editions. These are not fakes but can be misleading.

The most sought-after bears of this period are Steiff, worth at least £500. Those most likely to rise in price are Merrythought, because they have started producing limited editions and using real mohair. They are well-made and sought-after, commanding over £300, which is almost as much as Steiff. Limited editions of fewer than 5,000 should be a good investment for the future – although expect to hold your bear for at least ten years to make a profit.

Since 1980, accompanied by a growing interest from collectors, there has been an increase in hand-crafted bears and bears in human dress. The microchip has led to such novelties as musical bears with plastic hearts flashing in time to electronically generated lullabies.

GERMAN TEDDY BEARS

The most distinctive feature of later Steiff bears is the button and paper label. In 1953 the firm commemorated its 50 years of producing bears with Jackie the Jubilee Bear, designed as a bear cub with short, fat back legs and a chunky body.

The most obvious identifying marks are the pink stitch showing on the top of the dark thread of his nose and a small, dark-shaded area in the mohair plush on his tummy, representing his navel.

Jackie the Jubilee Bear was made in three heights: nearly 7 in (18 cm), 9 in (23 cm) and 13 in (33 cm) tall – in either beige or brown. The rarest, which are brown, are worth up to £500–600.

▲ STEIFF SIZE RANGE

Steiff had made several thousand miniature bears but in the 1970s the firm produced several hundred life-size, lifelike bears. The size affects the value of the bear up to a point but there are few people who have the space for a life-sized bear and thus the price does not rise accordingly after 30 in (76 cm) high. A life-sized polar bear by Steiff could be worth £2,000 while the small bear pictured, with a rare label and button, is worth only a little less, £800–1,200.

◀ SCHUCO
By the 1950s, Schuco was selling widely throughout North America, including Canada. The firm continued to be known for its miniature and mechanical bears until, as a result of the growth and success of the Japanese toy industry, the company finally went bankrupt in 1970. This typical 1950 beige bear is 19 in (48 cm) tall and has a short plush coat, stitched snout, glass eyes, a swivel-jointed body, a growler and short plush pads. The arms are no longer straight and the feet are noticeably bigger than those used on earlier bears. £200–400

▶ MINIATURES
Schuco miniatures were uniquely constructed with metal bodies. The earliest and smallest were only 2⅜in (6 cm) tall. Over the years they grew slightly larger and sturdier. This brown jointed bear is 2¾in (7 cm) tall and has a crown. It was given away as a promotional present at BP petrol stations between 1958 and 1960. £300–400

▶ YES/NO BEARS
These bears were very popular and come in various sizes, some having additional mechanical capabilities. This 1950s mohair bear is nearly 9in (29 cm) tall and has glass eyes. It nods or shakes its head when its tail is moved. £200–300

OTHER MAKERS

HERMANN – Since 1952 Hermann bears have borne tags and medallions declaring "Hermann Teddy Original" ("Teddy" is underlined). Limited editions, both of replica bears and new designs, include their Nostalgic bear range including a teddy-bear schoolroom in miniature. Limited editions of new designs are collectable. so long as less than 5,000. While 1960's Hermann's can be worth £400, limited editions are £200.

GRISLY – Grisly Spielwaren Fabrik was founded in Kircheimbolamdern, Germany by Karl Unfricht in 1954 and has expanded to employ several dozen workers. Some bears are made with acrylic plush and dralon. Bears made before 1974 have a button fastened to the chest with a bear on all fours, a needle and thread and the name 'Grisly'. In 1984 there was a special edition of 1,000 'Original Grisly Teddies'. £80–100 compared with £400–600 for Steiff and Hermann.

BRITISH TEDDY BEARS

While the larger teddy bear manufacturers were involved in take-over battles in the 1960s and 1970s and cheap bears flooded in from the Far East, smaller British producers were also beginning to proliferate. With so much variety available, collectors of antique bears of the future should look for limited editions.

Artist bears are so-named because they are made by bear lovers, often collectors themselves, who felt inspired to create their own individual designs. They are generally made to a good high standard and are increasingly very collectable. By the 1980s, whole colonies of artist bears had grown up such as the sleepy bears of Sue Quinn in Renfrewshire, Scotland (which go under the name of Dormouse Designs) or the Lilliputian Wareham Bears of Mary Hildesley in Dorset (which often appear on television). Probably the most popular is Little Mutt who has one leg shorter than the other and wears an orthopaedic boot. Prices range from £200–800.

◀ ▶ CHAD VALLEY

Chad Valley took over Chiltern in 1967 and was taken over by Palitoy in 1978. Unfortunately for collectors, all Chad Valley records and catalogues were destroyed, so dating is not always easy, although from 1953 the label shown on the pad read "...by appointment, Toy Makers to H.M. the Queen Mother". Chad Valley bears are noted for their soft bodies, since they were sometimes filled entirely with kapok. A particularly desirable range

was made in rainbow colours. The small bear pictured was made in 1953 and illustrates the change in later bears. The ears are placed flat on the head, rather than at an angle. The bulbous nose is stitched on vertically instead of horizontally, with arms longer and curved. £500–700

▶ DEAN'S

Dean's Rag Book Company Ltd moved to Rye in Sussex in the late 1950s, where production continued until 1982 despite a merger with Dean's Childsplay Toys and with Gwentoys whose factory was in Gwent, Wales, in 1972. One of Dean's chief designers was Silvia Wilgoss who was inspired by the bears at London Zoo to create this 1950s teddy which sits much like a real bear. He has painted black glass eyes with a black rubber surround, black rubber nose and lips, large ears, a hunch back, long arms and legs with beige rubber paws with claws. The rubber snout is attached in the form of a face mask under the mohair plush, which is quite unusual. Despite the fact that fur is missing and the rubber has deteriorated, the bear is still of considerable value. £600–800

MERRYTHOUGHT

ONE OF MERRYTHOUGHT'S
MOST POPULAR DESIGNS
WAS CHEEKY, INTRODUCED
IN 1957. HE CAME IN
SEVERAL SIZES AND
VERSIONS, SUCH AS THIS
ONE MADE IN ABOUT
1960 WHICH HAS NEW
PAW PADS. £300–400

The ears are very large,
attached on the side of
the head and have a bell
sewn inside them.

The eyes are big, made
from amber and black
plastic and set low on
the muzzle.

The mouth is stitched in
a wide smile.

The muzzle is made of
velvet. The nose is
stitched vertically.

Cheeky has large paws
and feet on which the
claws are stitched across
the plush into the felt.
The bottom of one foot
would be labelled:

"Merrythought
Ironbridge Shropshire
Made in England Regd.
Design". Be suspicious
of old labels appearing
on new pads.

▲ PLASTIC NOSES

From 1960 onwards, Chiltern
bears had black moulded plastic
noses. These were supposedly
modelled on the nose of a dog
rather than a bear.

▶ CHILTERN

Chiltern produced bears until
1967 when the firm was taken
over by Chad Valley. From
1967–78 bears were marked
Chiltern Chad Valley. Unshorn
faces and narrow, soft, velvet
feet with no reinforcements
are typical of later Chiltern
bears – although some have
canvas feet. This 1950 bear
is 24 in (61 cm) tall,
has glass eyes, a swivel-
jointed body and velvet
pads. £200–250

NORTH AMERICAN & OTHER TEDDY BEARS

Ideal grew into an international concern owning companies worldwide until it was eventually taken over in 1982 by C.B.S. Inc, which then stopped the firm's line of bear production. Other firms have continued to flourish in its stead. The new collectables among American bears are artist bears, which range from the realistic Den's Den animals of Vietnam veteran Denis Shaw to the much more traditional, but somewhat whimsically dressed, Kaleb Designs which are made by Barbara Wiltrout.

◀ **MASCOT BEARS**
Teddy bears have become favourite mascots. These four cotton plush bears belonged to students from the University of California who carried them as their rugby mascots during the 1960s.
£150–200 each

▶ **ANONYMOUS BEARS**
Such a large number of companies and individuals have produced teddy bears in recent years that many are impossible to identify, such as this 1970s bear with jointed knees. It is recognizably American, however, because of the ears and worth £30–50.

◀ **ADVERTISING BEARS**
By-products like this bear promoting Hershey's chocolate are very collectable. So are spin-offs from television programmes, like the Radar's teddy linked with M.A.S.H. Both were made in the 1970s. £60–80 each

▶ BERG BEARS

Made in Austria, Berg bears
are easily identifiable by their
trademark: "Berg Tiere mit
Herz", Mountain Animal Heart.
All carry a heart and a red
ribbon. They can be worth
as much as £100. This
example dates from
the 1950s. £50–60

▼ OTHER EUROPEAN BEARS

The best other European bears
are French, open-mouthed types
and Czechoslovakian unjointed
1950s bears (£30–300). This
1950s Dutch bear is made of
two-tone twill cotton and has
sideways-glancing eyes made
of tin. £65–70

▶ ROLY POLY BEARS

Roly Poly bears were the
perfect gift for small babies,
since they righted themselves
whenever they were knocked
over. This 1950s example,
which has the additional
benefit of a jingle, is American
and worth £48–55.

OTHER MAKERS

R. DAKIN AND COMPANY – Probably the
largest producer of soft toys in the world, the
firm began by importing hand-crafted toys
from Japan. A shipment of toy trains from
Japan in 1957 had velveteen soft toys as
packing material and the founder's son Roger
thought them attractive enough to sell.
Within a few years Dakin were selling
nothing else. In 1966 most of the Dakin
family were tragically killed in a plane crash,
but the firm went from strength to strength
producing every kind of bear and setting the
highest safety standards. No toxic materials
are used at any point in production and
massive stress tests make sure eyes are secure.
Pooky, the teddy owned by the cartoon cat
Garfield is a favourite and can be worth
£30–40. Almost half the bears produced by
Dakin are bought by adults for adults.

CELEBRITY BEARS

Bears have appeared in near-human form in children's stories for hundreds of years, from the Bruin of twelfth-century fables to the Three Bears of Goldilocks and nursery fame. It is not surprising then that literary and other celebrity bears turn up from time to time. The most famous storybook bear is Winnie the Pooh and he is so loved that if the original were to be offered at auction it would sell for upwards of £60,000.

◀ POOH BEAR
Winnie-the-Pooh was created by A.A. Milne in 1926, inspired by the Farnell bear purchased for his son Christopher Robin. Illustrator Ernest Shepard based Pooh on his own son's Steiff bear. 'Winnie' was a North American black bear in London Zoo: 'Pooh' was Christopher Robin's favourite swan. Disney Pooh bears are made in the United States by Sears, Roebuck and Company. This 1979 example does not have its original box, which lowers its value. £40–60

▶ RUPERT BEAR
The rather boy-like Rupert Bear was created in 1920 by cartoonist Mary Tourtel in the *Daily Express* and he grew in popularity under her successor Arthur Bestall and latterly a team of artists. He has human hands and feet and invariably wears a red jumper and yellow checked trousers with a matching scarf. He lives in the village of Nutwood and has extraordinary, magical adventures. This example was made in the UK by Bedy Toys in 1969 and is embossed with the copyright "Beaverbrook Newspapers". £25–35

▼ POPULAR ANNUALS
All celebrity bears have an assortment of related items. Books are among the most common but they are nevertheless collectable. These annuals are from the 1970s. If they are in good condition they can be worth £4–5 each.

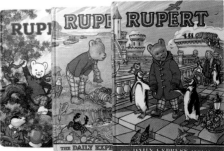

OTHER CELEBRITY BEARS

SMOKEY – In 1944, a bear appeared on posters for an American forest-fire prevention campaign. He was named after a legendary Assistant Chief of the New York City Fire Department 'Smokey Joe' Martin. One of the first licenced Smokey bears was made by Ideal in 1953 with a vinyl head, hands and feet and a brown plush body. By 1954 only the head was vinyl. He wore blue jeans, a special hat, silver badge and belt buckle and carried a blue plastic shovel.

The most valuable are £40–60.

SUPER TED – A bionic bear with zip-off fur coat, Super Ted first appeared in 1974. The hero of stories invented by Mike Read for his children, Super Ted could change into numerous disguises. The bear was designed by Read's wife Liz and made at a Welsh toy factory. American non-jointed versions, produced since 1985 by R. Dakin and Company in San Francisco, have Superman-style suits or an additional outer fur coat to be 'zipped' off. £35–45

▶ PADDINGTON

Paddington bear is named after the London railway station where he arrived as a stowaway from darkest Peru to live in Notting Hill, according to his creator Michael Bond. In fact he came from Selfridges where Bond was searching for a last-minute Christmas gift for his wife and thought the bear looked lonely. The story he devised was published in 1958 and illustrator Peggy Fortnum established the bear's shaggy appearance in bush hat, duffle coat and, later, Wellington boots. He is produced in the US by Eden and in Britain by Shirley Clarkson of Gabrielle Designs who began by making a couple for her children one Christmas. The 1972 Gabrielle Paddington bear pictured is worth £40–60.

◀ SOOTY

Sooty was so-called because his nose resembled a smudge of soot. The original bear was a hand-made puppet that entertainer Harry Corbet bought in 1948 from an elderly lady who had a novelty shop on the North Pier at Blackpool. Corbet was looking for something to amuse his three-year-old son Matthew. However, he was soon performing magic acts with the puppet and within four years they were starring on television. Small, replica Sooty puppets were designed and manufactured by Chad Valley and the early ones are worth £25–30. This 1960s example is made of plush. £15–20

Animal toys were nothing new when teddies were invented. But they were mostly carved in wood or sometimes made of cloth or composition. Rocking horses were an old favourite. So were Noah's Arks with pairs of painted animals occupying an impressive wooden ship. As travelling fairs and circuses popularized more exotic beasts, representative toys were equally in demand. But soft animal toys took off only after Margarete Steiff created her famous felt pincushions as gifts in 1880 (see page 48). Before long, Margarete had created a menagerie from pigs and donkeys to monkeys and camels. Other toymakers soon caught on: mainly teddy-bear manufacturers who had seamstresses and sewing-machines on hand. Children took to the animals which, like teddies, were cuddlier than traditional toys even if they incorporated clockwork movements or could be pulled along on wheels. Some were also bought by adults for adults. Television and films have made even exotic animals familiar and concern has escalated for their preservation. More and more animal soft toys are being produced worldwide every year, although the materials used are as varied as the quality. Steiff remain leading makers, producing both new designs and replicas of their original toys. The soft toys made by Steiff before the First World War are the most desirable, worth up to £100,000 – but examples by Chad Valley, Merrythought and Schuco are also in great demand. Prices generally are much lower than for teddy bears, but are likely to rise as more collectors turn to this new field.

STEIFF 1903-1949

No animal, from the farmyard to jungle, was too difficult for Steiff to recreate. Plush and velvet were the most usual materials being used – with excelsior stuffing and black boot-button or glass eyes. Some are exaggerated in a rather naive style, although most are very realistic – probably thanks to Margarete Steiff's nephew Richard, an art graduate and animal lover who became her chief designer. After teddy bears, the most sought after animals for collectors are jointed rabbits and elephants, with a value ranging from £30–300 depending on their size and age. The early Peter Rabbit by Steiff can reach £1,500 (see opposite).

▲ **ROCKING ELEPHANT**
This variation on the rocking horse was made by Steiff in 1908 and is particularly rare and in good condition. It has the typical black boot-button eyes, realistic features and Steiff button in one ear. It is covered in beige hessian, like a soft-toy, and could be rocked or pulled along. £800–1200

BEWARE
Watch out for genuine buttons added to incorrect animals. Take care not to confuse limited edition Steiff replicas with originals as the former are sometimes distressed deliberately. Damaged fur reduces value by as much as three-quarters.

▲ SKITTLES

Skittles in one form or another have been a favourite game for centuries. Made in plush, velvet and wool, they were an early version of the soft toy, devised by Margarete Steiff in the mid 1880s with a bear, a precursor of the teddy (see pages 48–51), as the kingpin. This 1908 group of nine animals, all on circular wooden bases, are each 8 in (20 cm) tall except for the bear which is just over 10 in (25 cm) thanks to his red felt crown. The pig, rabbit, three dogs, cat and elephant are velvet, the lamb is wool and the bear is plush. Every animal has a Steiff button and only one dog-collar is missing. £6,000–8,000

▼ ▶ PETER RABBIT

(left) A 1905 Steiff Peter Rabbit with elephant trademark on sole of slipper. £1,500–2,000 (right) A 1904 rare lambswool-covered Peter with blank Steiff button in ear. £2,000–3,000

▲ MUSICAL BONZO

This 1930 musical dog is a variation of Bonzo, the bull terrier pup created by Chad Valley and originally drawn in *The Daily Sketch*. Bonzo leapt to fame in 1920 when King George and Queen Mary were amused at a British Industries Fair by an entertainer dressed in a Bonzo suit. About £500

OTHER SOFT TOYS 1903–1949

Steiff animal soft toys were selling so well that other makers quickly began to imitate its products. In Germany numerous small companies produced a range of different animals in cloth, felt, leather and plush; although in America the teddy-bear craze became so great that until the 1930s there was little room for manufacturing anything else. Dean's and Farnell, Chad Valley and Merrythought were among the first makers in Britain, along with Eisenmann & Co who were top importers from Germany. Look out for animals from children's literature, especially Beatrix Potter. When the maker cannot be identified, it is worth looking out for quality in the material, design and stitching. Some animals by other manufacturers were as good as Steiff, but are much cheaper to buy now.

▶ **DEAN'S**

Dean's Rag Book Band is a particularly rare and sought-after group. This 1930 example includes two white rabbits, two gold-plush teddy bears and two rubber-faced monkeys, each 19in (48cm) tall and wearing a popular band-player's outfit, all with an instrument and five with chairs. £2,000–3,000

◀ **LITERARY FIGURES**

Dean's spotted the popularity of certain characters in children's literature and immediately started making soft toys of such animals as Peter Rabbit from the Beatrix Potter books. Tatters (the hospital pup with an upraised, bandaged paw) was issued in 1928 and Dismal Desmond (who was first manufactured as a pitiful-looking Dalmatian in 1923) was supplemented in 1933 by a Cheerful Desmond. The most valuable characters are Bonzo, Dismal Desmond, Bambi and Peter Rabbit. This Desmond, which was made in the 1930s, would fetch £100–150.

▶ **KIDDIELAND**

Kiddieland, registered in 1911, was one of the trademarks of Eisenmann & Co of Fuerth, Bavaria and London, established by Joe and Gabriel Eisenmann in 1881. Prior to the First World War, Joe Eisenmann was nicknamed the King of the Toy Trade in London since he controlled the bulk of the imports to Britain. This 1918 toy is identified by a label bearing "Tubby" and "I Turn My Eyes". Owing to its charm, label and good condition, this one is worth £30–40.

WHAT TO
LOOK FOR
- Cats with green eyes.
- Rabbits and hares
with yellow eyes.
- Dogs like a dachshund,
poodle or sheepdog.
- Characters from
film and television if
they are in soft material
and jointed, and also
have their label
and name showing.

▶ **CHAD VALLEY**
Oolo was the girlfriend of
Bonzo in the books of the
same name. She has an
identification button in her
ear and, although many were
made in the 1930s, few have
survived. Due to rarity, she is
very sought after. £400–600
Bonzo and Oolo toys came in
various sizes. The larger tend to
be more expensive. Limbs can
be either rigid or swivel and
moving limbs are worth more.

◀ **UNIDENTIFIABLE
MAKERS**
The importance of a famous
name is obvious in the value
ascribed to this 7 in- (18 cm-)
high, felt-covered clockwork
horse. Because of the key
and felt saddle, it must be
continental and made in the
1930s. Its origin could be
Germany or France. Were it
made by Steiff, it would be
worth more. £40–45

▶ **FARNELL**
This monkey is one of Farnell's
Alpha toys, made of pressed
felt in about 1930. In mint
condition and with glass eyes,
it would be worth £200–250.
The more usual Farnell soft
toys are rabbits, dogs, foxes
and birds – with prices ranging
from £50–500. For some
reason, monkeys are not as
popular as other animals as soft
toys and this is reflected in the
value they fetch.

STEIFF 1950–1980s

In the 1950s, Steiff began to make a number of animals which were life-sized or sometimes even larger than life. These ranged from giant rabbits to realistic dogs, crocodiles and kangaroos. Unlike the small Steiff animals they were unjointed. Eyes were wooden or glass. All are rare but the most desirable are rabbits, elephants and pigs, which can be worth £400–600. Steiff have continued as major producers of all sorts of animals and any which are in good condition, preferably still with the box they came in, are likely to steadily increase in value over the years to come.

▲ NOAH'S ARK

Creating your own Noah's Ark is a pastime enjoyed by both children and collectors, although ark and animals can be bought as a set. This collection of some four dozen creatures including okapi, elephants, monkeys, lions, penguins and tortoises dates mostly from the 1950s. Many have swing tags and most have a button and label in the ear. Steiff concentrated on the animals children saw most in zoos. £2,000–3,000

▶ IDENTIFICATION

Steiff labelling in conjunction with the button changed over the years. From 1950 to 1970, the button was chrome, the name was first written in script on a yellow label and a place was designated for the price. From 1970, the number on the label referring to the animal's posture, covering, height and outfit included an oblique in place of a comma and the button was brass, as in the label pictured. In 1980 a yellow-and-white woven label was introduced, and black-and-white one was produced for use

on limited editions. It is fairly common to find various small Steiff animals at Doll and Teddy Bear Fairs, especially in Germany where a collectable example could be bought in the mid-1990s for as little as £30.

REPRODUCTIONS

Such is the demand for early Steiff designs that in the 1980s the company began to make limited-edition replicas of other animals as well as bears and many dealers sell reproductions as well as originals. They can complement each other, but take care not to confuse them. Reproductions are made to be collectable and are traditionally manufactured and stuffed with excelsior. They are airbrushed with fine details to make them appear as realistic as possible and mostly range from just over 5 in (13 cm) to 24 in (61 cm) tall. Thus a charming replica 1930 terrier called Rattler with a head that moves when his tail is turned, made in an edition of 4,000 in 1992, might cost £95 new. Second-hand, he might be worth £50 but as stocks run out his value is likely to rise by £20.

▼ **PUPPETS**
Glove puppets became fashionable following the success of the puppet bear Sooty on television. In the early 1950s, Steiff made many glove puppets.

Penguins were a particularly suitable shape for puppets and this one dates from the 1960s. Keep in mind that good condition is essential for recent soft toys. £25–30

▼ **TOP ANIMALS**
The value of later animals depends on several factors. Good condition is essential and 1950s toys are generally preferable to 1960s or later. The average size is around 9 in (23 cm) tall or long, and larger creatures are usually more costly. But rarity and attractiveness can make others more desirable.

Thus in the line-up illustrated below, the 1950 buffalo is worth only £22–35 compared with the more appealing 1948 lamb at £48–60. The amusing 1958 owl is worth about £38–50 and the pig, always a favourite, is also worth £38–50 – despite dating more recently from 1960. Pigs, owls, rabbits and dogs are the most popular types of animals for

collectors and therefore tend to be higher in price. This is a curious hierarchy of preferences which would be interesting for some pychologist to explain. Why some creatures have so much more appeal than others is an intriguing mystery. For some reason, toy dogs have become more common than toy cats since the 1950s.

OTHER SOFT TOYS 1950–1980s

American toymakers made up for lost time in the production of soft toys, although the competition from the Far East has been increasingly strong, especially for cheaper examples. North American animals to look out for are known characters inspired by the film industry. In England, toys by the old established firms such as Dean's are the most desirable. The most valuable later soft toys are African safari-type animals, like lions and zebras, and polar bears. Other countries known for soft toys include Australia (thanks to its real-life kangaroos and koala bears) and Canada (with its grizzly bears and a spoof furry trout).

◀ ZOO-TIME

The popularity of new arrivals and births at London Zoo led to the creation of toys like this white polar bear mother and cub by Dean's, based in Merton, London. Made in the 1950s, the toy is identified by a swing tag at the neck: "Dean's Hygienic Toys". The mother, 19 in (48 cm) tall, is made of white mohair and has a leather nose; the cub is in wool with a black embroidered nose.
£500–600

▼ WALT DISNEY

Films by Walt Disney have led to a wealth of soft-toy stars. Among the most desirable are the nursery animal friends of Christopher Robin in the stories of Winnie-the-Pooh written by A.A. Milne. The most sought-after makers are Chad Valley and Merrythought. But even if of unknown make, they are worth collecting. In this group Pooh is the favourite, a 1960s version made of flannel being the most desirable. But Piglet and Eeyore are still sought after. Pooh £50–60, Piglet and Eeyore £26–28.

▲ EDEN TOY

The American firm Eden Toy Inc is particularly noted for a number of character animals, including its own version of Paddington Bear. Peter Rabbit has become similarly popular thanks to the publication around the world of Beatrix Potter's stories. Eden toys can be worth £30–40. Due to charm, this 1960s version of Peter with his ingenuous expression wearing his unmistakable blue coat is worth £28–40.

▶ **COLOUR**
In recent years the use of inappropriate colours for animals, like Chad Valley's rainbow series for bears, has become more frequent. In the case of these two squirrels, both light and dark brown are fairly realistic. But the colour has a distinct bearing on value. Although the darker squirrel dates from 1960, it is worth as much as the lighter shade from the 1950s. £40–50

◀ **JAPANESE COMPETITION**
Japanese soft toys have flooded the Western market since the 1970s when this plush velvet lion was made. While some are expensive, this lion is at the other end of the scale and worth comparatively little. £10–15

WHAT TO LOOK FOR
• Named makers, as most animals of any value have labels.
• Known animal characters. These are the most likely to rise in value, especially if they are favourites from the world of films.
• Cuddliness and cuteness beyond what is usual.

BEWARE
Do not expect every soft toy animal to increase rapidly in value. Apart from the maker or label and quality of materials and workmanship, the design must be attractive and condition excellent. Other Far Eastern countries besides Japan are now manufacturing millions of toys each year.

◀ **MYSTERY MAKERS**
Excessive numbers of soft toys produced in a wide price range has left many unidentifiable. Mystery makes, however, if particularly unusual designs or those of high quality, may well be the antiques of tomorrow. A 1960s cotton plush 9in- (23cm-) high dog is still a snip in good condition at £5–10, a slightly bigger and more unusual camel from 1–3ft (30-90cm) would be worth £10 –15.

BEAR-RELATED ITEMS 1900–1980s

The craze for teddy bears has inevitably led to a wide variety of related items being produced – bear accessories or artefacts represent bears at both work and play.

Postcards with bears were hugely popular at the beginning of the century and bear annuals proliferated with the growing number of famous bear characters. Pottery firms cashed in on the fashion with tea services for children featuring bears and top jewellers and clothes designers picked up the bear motif, as did greetings card manufacturers. The affection indicated by a teddy bear further led to the adoption of bear-related items as love tokens.

▲ ▶ POTTERY
Many leading pottery factories, such as Wedgwood who made children's services, spotted the sales potential of the teddy bear. Sadly, many pieces were broken and whole services are very rare. Watch for chips and cracks. The most valuable examples are plates and bowls with a centre bear and maker's marks on the reverse. This teddy bear porringer is worth £60. Baby's plate £100–200; cups and saucers £30–40 each; plates £30–35 each.

◀ GAMES AND PUZZLES
Games, and especially jigsaws, provided a perfect opportunity for jumping on the bear bandwagon. This example by Victory is very typically sentimental for the 1940s. The overall condition must be good and check also that the game or jigsaw is all there, as any missing pieces can reduce the value to virtually nothing. This one is worth up to £60.

▶ **FASHION ACCESSORIES**
Teddy bears were taken on
board by the fashion industry
from the beginning of this
century. The warmth of bear's
fur made them perfect for muffs,
as in the case of these two
examples. One is a very early
muff (the maker unknown but
probably American), the other is
a 1970 Merrythought Cheeky
bear muff. Left: £500–600
Right: £150–200

▼ **ROMANCE**
Stories and songs such as the
Teddy Bears' Picnic have been
exploited widely. This 1990
musical picnic is a typically
sentimental scene aimed at older
collectors. £100–150

◀ **DUAL PURPOSE**
Teddy bears sometimes had a
dual purpose. Some held
lipsticks, others were perfume
holders. For this reason they
were often small, such as this
3½in (9 cm) Schuco bear with a
compact and lipstick holder in
the neck, worth £300–400.
Look for a belly with mirror on
one side, powder on the other.

WHAT TO LOOK FOR
● Any items associated with celebrity bears are
collectable, especially so if they relate to a famous story.
● Surprises such as dual-purpose bears. These are
increasing in value as curiosities.
● Series of books in top condition.
Better still, look for first editions.
● Whole children's tea services – particularly those
by famous makers.
● Original illustrations for well-known stories, such as
Ernest Shephard's Pooh drawings.
● Early 20th-century postcards depicting bears, especially
novelty and pop-up cards.
● Bears on biscuit tins and other ephemera which are in
the best condition.

PART 5

DOLL FILE

ABOVE A KÄMMER & REINHARDT BISQUE DOLL,
MOULD NO. 117, C.1911. £4,000–5,000

LEFT AN EMILE JUMEAU 'A' SERIES BISQUE DOLL,
FRENCH, C.1880. £20,000–25,000

Carved wooden dolls were made in forest regions throughout Europe in the seventeenth century and earlier. Known as 'babies' because they were children's playthings, they were normally dressed as adults. Sold at big fairs such as St Bartholomew's in London, they are often called 'Bartholomew's babies'. Few have survived. Values vary from a few hundred pounds to hundreds of thousands. The pair illustrated (opposite) may have been for private pantomimes for those in fashionable society who could neither afford the travelling players employed for court masques nor wished to involve outsiders in acting out treasonable ideas.

The first English doll-carver known by name was William Higgs, who probably began working in London in the late-seventeenth century and could have made these dolls. Higgs's dolls were the subject of a trial in 1733 after an employee stole several of them. In court Higgs declared: "I can swear to my work for there's never a man in England that makes such babies as me". His wooden-jointed 'babies' were made on his furniture lathe, painted by his apprentices and dressed by his wife. He sold them for 2½ pence each and many were sold in Whitechapel, an area of London famous for making toys and dolls.

One of the most famous doll collectors was Marianne Bodmer 1928–86), a German sportswoman and picture-reporter who married Swiss industrialist and art-lover Peter Bodmer. She died before she could realize her plan for a museum to house her collection – which included many very fine wooden dolls.

WOODEN DOLLS I

The earliest known group of wooden dolls is English, and these date from the last 20 years of the 17th century. Twenty-three have come to light with a similar appearance and are probably by the same maker. They are so meticulously carved and painted it is likely that they were intended for adults. A selection of them is shown on pages 86–7. At least six of those known are in public collections, including London's Victoria & Albert Museum. Others are kept in the Legoland Museum in Denmark), The Doll Museum in Anaheim, California and the Bethnal Green Museum of Childhood and British Museum, both in London.

WHAT TO LOOK FOR
- At this time men wore even more splendid fashions than ladies. Lord Clapham has narrow breeches in silver with a matching waistcoat and scarlet wool coat (red was very much a favourite French baroque colour).
- Cravats were introduced in 1690 and silk stockings were considered a vital part of fashionable dress.
- The wig beneath Lord Clapham's tricorne is typical, since men shaved their heads for reasons of both hygiene and comfort.
- Wigs had become so extravagant by the turn of the century that hats were carried simply as an accessory.

LORD AND LADY CLAPHAM

THESE DOLLS ARE SO-NAMED BECAUSE THEIR FIRST-KNOWN OWNER IS THOUGHT TO HAVE BEEN A MEMBER OF THE JACKSON FAMILY WHO LIVED IN CLAPHAM, LONDON. JOHN JACKSON WAS THE FAVOURITE NEPHEW OF THE DIARIST SAMUEL PEPYS AND JOHN'S DAUGHTER FRANCES MARRIED ONE OF THE COCKERELL FAMILY THROUGH WHOSE DESCENDANTS THE PAIR WERE HANDED DOWN. THE DOLLS ARE EACH 22 IN (56 CM) TALL AND EXQUISITELY DETAILED. THEY ARE UNDOUBTEDLY INTENDED TO REPRESENT KING WILLIAM AND QUEEN MARY AND ARE PROBABLY THE WORLD'S MOST VALUABLE PAIR OF DOLLS. £200,000–300,000

The highly fashionable fontange head-dress (see page 88) was not usually tied under the chin.

The dolls are seated on their own fine chairs.

This three-cornered hat is made of black felt with silver braid and sequins and bears the maker's name inside:

"T Bourdillon, Hosier and Hatter to His Majesty, No 14 Russell St, Covent Garden".

Wired swivel necks enabled the dolls to turn their heads, simulating conversation.

The gown is of white Chinese export silk damask trimmed with English bobbin lace and silver braid.

The wedding ring is gold.

The mask has a bead mouthpiece to hold it in place. Disguise was affected for anonymity at society gatherings.

The shoes are of white silk brocade on silver.

The leather shoes are hand sewn.

The miniature sword and scabbard are exquisitely worked.

WOODEN DOLLS II

The bodies of wooden dolls are skittle-like in shape. This was a convenient shape to make on a lathe since it was similar to a chair leg, and turners are recorded as having produced dolls from Shakespearean times onwards. The arms and legs are attached separately and the legs have peg joints. The wired and padded upper arms end in wooden wrists with rather large hands, carefully carved with long fingers.

Although there are references to dressed dolls from the 14th century onward in paintings and books, original clothes are, for obvious reasons, hard to find and if the doll still wears them it boosts its value enormously.

The clothes of wooden dolls reflected the contemporary 17th-century fashions. Ladies wore their bodices cut as low as possible, with sleeves elbow length or shorter and the sleeves of a lace chemise peeping out beneath. Skirts were bell-shaped and sewn onto the bodice. A tiny waist was essential. This was achieved in real life by wearing a tight corset and steel busk forming a vertical line from below the breasts to the bottom of the torso. It was uncomfortable but supportive while standing for long periods at court ceremonies. Outer garments were usually in a contrasting colour in satin or velvet.

◀ LADY ELTON
Lady Elton, as this doll is known, has a rigid neck, with a head-dress that is the precursor to a full fontange (see page 88). She also has fashionable beauty spots and lavish clothes made of original silk and satin. This doll is in the Legoland Museum.
£80,000–100,000

▶ MODEL FIGURE
This is a particularly large doll at nearly 24 in (60 cm) tall, with typical late 17th-century clothes embroidered with the initials "LG". She has a wired neck with protruding wire at the base of the spine with which to turn the head, but no fontange.
£80,000–100,000+

▲ REAL-HAIR WIG
This doll has a swivel neck and the remains of a real-hair wig. But she has no beauty spot and her dress and headwear are not original. £60,000–80,000

▶ **PLAIN JANE**
Although less fashion-conscious
than some, this doll with a
swivel neck, flaxen hair and
silk and silver-gilt trimmings
nevertheless sold at an auction
house in London in 1991 for
£71,500.

BEWARE
These dolls are so rare
that the chances of
finding one are very slight
indeed. Nevertheless, it is
possible. Be careful not to
be persuaded that you
have spotted one just
because you want to.
Seek all the proof you can
of the doll's provenance.

◀ **ORIGINAL CLOTHES**
Original silk and satin clothes
with a white muslin bonnet are
an important feature of this doll,
whose history is unknown. She
has a rigid neck and somewhat
crudely carved ears.
£80,000–100,000

▲ **RIGID NECK**
This doll is 15¾in (40 cm)
tall, with a rigid neck and
no beauty spot. Her silk dress
is original and she has a later
wig which has been placed over
the original nailed-on wig. Her
bonnet is original and has been
silk-edged in metal thread.
£40,000–60,000

WHAT TO LOOK FOR
● Shape – could the body
double as part of a chair leg?
● Head – is the head dis-
proportionately large
or appropriately sized for
the rest of the body?
● Features – do they look
true to life or a caricature
of a real woman? If so, it
could mean that the doll was
commissioned and carved to
resemble the lady of the
house.
● Hands – are the hands
realistically carved, albeit
over-large?

WOODEN DOLLS III

◀ FONTANGE

The fontange, an elaborate ribboned and wired head-dress, was named after Mademoiselle de Fontanges. One of Louis XIV's mistresses in the 1690s, she went out hunting with the King and, following his attentions, found her hair in disarray. So she tied it up in a topknot with one of her garters. The next day all the other ladies at Court adopted the fashion and began to improve on it, and before long the style spread. Lady Clapham's arrangement (left) is incorrectly tied under the chin (see opposite for full effect). Dolls with this head-dress have swivel necks.

▶ BEAUTY SPOTS

Beauty spots or patches are typical on late-17th century dolls. In 1660 the diarist Samuel Pepys wrote: "My wife seemed very pretty today, it being the first time I had given her leave to wear a black patch". Pretending to have a 'mole' to offset beauty began in classical times. Patches were, of course, a convenient way of covering up smallpox scars. They became fashionable at the French Court in the 17th century and reached England when Charles I married Henrietta Maria in 1625. They were painted onto dolls but in reality were usually made of black silk impregnated with adhesive and came in a variety of shapes, such as half-moons, stars, hearts, cupids and even a

coach and horses. Different meanings were conveyed by the position in which patches were fixed: stars at the corner of the mouth, for example, being particularly suggestive. The larger beauty spots were called 'assassins' for their supposedly devastating effect.

▼ HAIR

Real hair was often used on wooden dolls. It was attached to a linen cap which was nailed to the head. Faces were mostly round and rouged, while mouths have an enigmatic Mona Lisa quality. The neck is wide and the shoulders squared.

◀ EYES

The eyes of a 17th-century wooden doll sometimes have unusual white spots to accentuate the pupil. Both eyes and eyebrows were usually painted on. Some of the eyes of 17th-century dolls have a single line above to denote the upper lid. Others have a line below as well. The eyebrows are usually a single line with dashes above and below the line giving a herringbone effect. Fixed black eyes without pupils and made of glass were more common in the 18th century. They tend to be duller and can render the doll less valuable, since eyes are probably the most important facial feature and can contribute greatly to the doll's appeal.

PAPIER-MÂCHÉ DOLLS

Scarce evidence remains of early papier-mâché dolls. They were popular as a cheaper alternative to wooden dolls and the earliest reference to them is in mid-16th century France, where dolls were made of *carton-pierre*, a mixture of clay, paper and plaster.

These two 17th-century British dolls are among the earliest surviving examples that are not religious figures. Sold with the Clapham pair (see pages 84–5) they were last in the collection of the late Marianne Bodmer (see page 84). They probably came from the same workshop as the Claphams as the fontanges and hands are similarly worked – so they may also have been made around 1690. Only the head and shoulders were carefully painted. The legs of one are wooden, jointed at hip and knee with a metal hook to allow the doll to sit or stand; the other has crude papier-mâché legs and feet. Wooden hands were attached by cloth or wire arms. The value of these dolls lies in their condition, original exquisite clothes, and having been in the Bodmer Collection. £40,000–60,000 each

MODELS OR PLAYTHINGS?

THESE ELEGANTLY DRESSED AND WELL PRESERVED DOLLS MAY HAVE BEEN MADE AS MODELS FOR THE FASHION TRADE RATHER THAN FOR CHILDREN.

The dress is of gold silk damask with sack back over an embroidered petticoat, a ribbed petticoat and a white shift.

The wig is of mohair.

The elaborate white spotted muslin fontange is identical to that of Lady Clapham (see page 85).

The eyes are carefully painted.

The hidden upper arms are of cloth.

The silver thread stomacher is very intricately worked.

The wooden forked hands are similar to those of Lady Clapham.

The leather-heeled slippers are of blue velvet.

◀ **PAINTED FEATURES**
This 17-in (43-cm) doll has painted features and her fontange is similar to Lady Clapham's. Her pink and white spotted yellow silk petticoat and robe with pink cuffs and flounces is worn over an embroidered silk shift and white undershift. Her hidden arms are made of wire. She also wears a silver thread stomacher.

Most important wooden dolls date from the 18th century. Well carved and elaborately dressed, they were the playthings of children of wealthy families. English dolls were particularly noted for their finesse and are often referred to as Queen Anne dolls in the US. Those which have survived with original clothes and wigs as well as original limbs and paint are generally the most valuable and the larger the doll, the better.

The quality of dollmaking deteriorated towards the end of the century, chiefly as a result of imports flooding in from German makers and the increase in manufacture of papier-mâché and wax dolls. The cheaper German dolls were the precursors of the fairground peg dolls or penny woodens.

Unusually, English wooden dolls were completed by one maker. In Europe, where the guilds' traditions were stronger, several different craftsmen and seamstresses would be involved in carving, painting and dressing one doll. Ivory dolls were also made in various European countries, although mostly for religious purposes, and a number were imported as souvenirs from the Far East as trade increased, especially with China. These dolls were often exquisitely carved and dressed and are now highly sought after. The carved ivory ones are so beautifully detailed that they are true collectors' items. English wooden novelty dolls in unusual garb, or those which were satirical or erotic – sometimes made to poke fun at the monarchy – are also increasing in value.

WOODEN DOLLS I

Subtle changes appear between early- and late-eighteenth-century dolls which can affect their value. The size and attractiveness of the doll, a known history and inclusion in an important collection all add to the worth of a particular doll. The dolls on these two pages all come from the Bodmer Collection (see page 84) and as such their value is enhanced.

◀ **YORKSHIRE LINEAGE**
This 1735 doll, 29 in (74 cm) tall, has a finely painted gessoed face (with a damaged tip of the nose) and was owned by a Yorkshire family during the 19th century.
£40,000–60,000

▶ **SIZE: LARGE**
Dating from 1735, this doll has no history before its inclusion in the Bodmer Collection. A large doll – almost 30 in (76 cm) tall – with a carefully carved and cleverly jointed body, she even has her original shoes.
£40,000–60,000

◀ **SIZE: SMALL**
This 14 in (35 cm) doll dates from 1740. Her typical features are a flax wig and eyes without pupils.
£10,000–15,000

▲ **RESTORATION**
Produced in 1790, this doll is smaller than average at under 12 in (30 cm) tall. She has typical features, but also unusual tiny block hands. Her dress, although not original, is particularly elaborate. At some time she has been restored, which does reduce her value. £3,000–4,000

◀ **REAL-HAIR WIG**
This 26 in- (66 cm-) tall doll from 1735 again has no history prior to the Bodmer Collection. Typical of the period, she has a nailed auburn real-hair wig, rouged cheeks and dotted eyelashes. £20,000–30,000

▶ **GROVE BABY**
Dating from 1782 and known as the 'Grove Baby' (see below), this doll is 20 in (51 cm) tall, with blue glass eyes and a nailed wig of real hair. She comes with her own box inscribed with date, a letter signed "Jane A. Grove" and a list of extra "Baby's Things", including nightdresses and a handkerchief initialled "D". She is plainly dressed and rather crudely carved, but was also in the Bodmer sale. £4,000–5,000

▲ **FANCY DRESS**
This doll was also made in 1790 and measures nearly 17 in (43 cm) tall. Note the typical rouged cheeks, black glass eyes, dotted lashes, nailed wig and cloth upper arms. Although she is missing a finger, the fancy outfit is a bonus. Unfortunately she has been restored on the face and the value is lower than if she had been left in her original state. £7,000–8,000

WOODEN DOLLS II

Developments in fashion through the 18th century are especially important in helping to date a doll, although the original clothes may have worn out and outfits dating from the 18th century may have been replaced over the years. A characteristic feature of the Rococo (1730–1789) epoch was its complete absence of moderation. Skirts grew wider and then elliptical, supported with hoops, to exaggerate a tiny waist. Silk with flower motifs or heavy brocade was the most popular fabric. The neckline was low and shoes were delicate.

▶ PANNIÈRE GOWNS
This beautifully carved, 19-in (48-cm) tall doll made in 1735 has a well-carved body with formed breasts, tapered waist, squared hips and jointed legs. Her magnificent gold satin gown with matching shoes and hat was fashionable in the first half of the 18th century and named for the baskets carried by pack animals. The lower legs have been replaced, as new wood and jointing reveals.
£15,000–20,000

▲ SERENE FACE
Dating from 1735 and notable for her serene expression, this doll has a round face with painted, highly rouged cheeks, painted black eyes, irises with two white dots, well-carved ears and the remains of a silk beauty spot on her forehead. With her splayed hands and long fingers, protruding bosom and rounded hips with peg-jointed hips and knees, the quality is reminiscent of the very best 17th-century dolls.
£35,000–40,000

◀ SWIVEL HEADS
The swivel head of this 1750 British doll is attached by a metal rod to a ring in her bottom. She has painted features with a well defined nose and long fingers, but a poorly carved torso and block feet. The replaced dress and general damage (one foot and four fingers are missing) lowers the value, but the rare swivel mechanism makes her desirable.
£6,000–8,000

ELEGANT STYLE

ORIGINALLY AN EXPENSIVE DOLL MADE C.1759, SHE IS MADE FROM TOP-QUALITY MATERIALS. NOTE THE INTRICATE JOINTING OF THE UNDRESSED DOLL. THE WORK OF A MASTER DOLLMAKER IS IN THIS CASE COMPLEMENTED BY AN OUTFIT CREATED BY A TOP, POSSIBLY EVEN A ROYAL, DRESSMAKER. £15,000–20,000

The typical inserted glass eyes are elongated in opaque glass. They have little discernible white and no pupil.

The eyebrows are feather painted.

Pink spots highlight the cheeks.

The face is gesso covered.

The thin mouth has a rosebud centre.

The waist is still quite narrow, helping to date this doll to the mid-18th century.

She is elaborately dressed in brocaded silk-satin and chenille lace in early rococo styles with a wide skirt, pinched waist and deep décolleté.

WOODEN DOLLS III

A doll's shape can indicate the date of manufacture. Earlier wooden bodies tend to have a tapered waist and a thin neck with a proportionally small head. Towards the end of the 18th century, dolls had thicker necks, more sloping shoulders, a higher bust and no waist

(see pages 36–7). This may have been as a result of changing fashions, but the shape was probably also easier to produce. The later shape is less desirable, being an indication of how wooden dolls deteriorated in quality in the 19th century.

▶ DISC JOINTS
Pegged disc joints at the shoulder, elbow, hip and knee were often used in the 17th, 18th and 19th centuries to enable the doll to move. They were carved and turned in the same way as a hinged table leg. This 1760 doll has an unusually long body in proportion to her height of 15 in (38 cm).
£13,000–15,000

WHAT TO LOOK FOR
● Facial features should be delicately painted with softly shaded cheeks. Earlier dolls may have beauty spots.
● The head and torso was usually made in one piece with arms and legs attached by leather straps.
● Jointed elbows, hips and knees and carved fingers and toes are a good indication of top quality.

◀ RED CHEEKS
This 1790 doll is fairly tall at 26 in (66 cm), has a rounded face, rouged cheeks, inserted pupil-less eyes and brush-stroked lashes and brows. She has unusually accentuated hips and heavy thighs, and is jointed at hip and knee. She has block feet and cloth upper and wooden lower arms, ending in long fingers. Her striped muslin dress is from a later date.
£3,000–5,000

▲ VISIBLE HEART
This doll, from 1800, is more crudely carved than the other examples shown here. She has straight legs, block feet, stump

hands and wooden arms attached by means of a wire round the torso. The red heart attached to her dress is a pin-cushion.
£3,000–5,000

IVORY DOLLS

Ivory dolls have long been made in China and the Far East. Increasing trade with the Orient in the 18th century made the dolls fashionable in Europe, although in China ivory was not particularly valuable. Today they are very collectable and although ivory stains with age and may have cracked because of a dry atmosphere, these factors do not necessarily detract from the value. Ivory dolls were often made for religious purposes and were also carved by church carpenters for crèches. Others were recycled as children's playthings.

▶ CHINESE LADY
Made in China towards the end of the 18th century, this doll's ivory head and neck are attached with a peg to the wooden body which has disc joints at shoulder, elbow, hip and knee. The lashes above her inserted brown eyes and her wig are of real hair. The ivory hands and feet have carved nails. Crack lines on cheek and neck are slight.
£12,000–15,000

▼ CHINESE MAN
This late-18th century figure is dressed in his original rust-red silk coat with flower-embroidered cuffs. Made in China, the body is of paper-covered thin wooden slats, the head and forearms of ivory. The head is well sculpted with long pierced ears and carved hair. Long fingers have pointed nails. The value is high despite some crazing.
£12,000–15,000

◀ GERMAN QUEEN
Possibly made in southern Germany c.1760, this 13in-(33 cm-) doll has a swivelling, ivory head on a wooden body, disc-joints at shoulders, elbows, hips and knees, and detailed ivory hands and feet. The head is well carved and she has real grey hair. The cream satin panels and the crown could date from when the waist was carved at a later date, as this queen is likely to have been a king originally.
£8,000–10,000

NOVELTY DOLLS

Dolls were frequently made either for special festivities – or to honour or satirize certain celebrities and professions. Physical and most especially sexual oddity was a sure fairground attraction and general source of entertainment. Religion also played a very prominent role in 18th-century society and members of holy orders were venerated and admired. Many such dolls were, however, no more than inexpensive novelties and as a consequence only a few of the better quality examples have survived until today.

THE HAPPY COUPLE

THIS RARE PAIR OF 11 IN (28 CM) BRITISH EROTIC DOLLS, JOINTED AND WITH SWIVEL HEADS, ARE DATED C.1770. UNUSUALLY FOR WOODEN DOLLS, THEY HAVE OPEN MOUTHS AND PAINTED BLUE EYES. THEY ARE HERMAPHRODITE DOLLS WITH FULLY CARVED GENITALIA AND THE COUPLE ARE PROBABLY A SATIRE ON GEORGE III (1760–1820) AND QUEEN CHARLOTTE. SUCH A PAIR WOULD HAVE BEEN TYPICAL IN REPRESENTING THE ANTI-MONARCHIST SENTIMENT THAT WAS COMMON IN HUMANIST CIRCLES AT THE TIME, AND WOULD PROBABLY HAVE BEEN SPECIALLY COMMISSIONED. BOTH DOLLS ARE BADLY WORN, WITH ELEGANT BUT DISTRESSED CLOTHES AND FADED FACIAL PAINT. £12,000–15,000

Serious expressions on their faces may cover repressed sexual desires.

Swivel necks enable the pair to 'converse'.

He wears his original pink waistcoat, brocaded coat and silk breeches but is probably missing a wig and hat. In spite of his being King his dress is sober, in keeping with the German male fashion of the time.

The detailed jewellery is appropriate for the Queen.

The carved bosom is accentuated.

Carved genitalia are hidden beneath clothes.

She wears her original muslin and lace underskirts, open robe of brocaded silk, ruched edging and matching bonnet – all fashion appropriate for mimicking the Queen.

BEWARE

Just because a doll is described as 18th century this does not mean it is worth thousands of pounds. It may be poorly carved and crudely painted, and its costume may have been run up last year. Be sure to examine the body under the clothes, removing them where possible, and watch out for synthetic materials.

▶ **NUN**

This British wooden doll is dressed in the original heavy brown wool habit of a lay sister, probably of the Order of the Dames of Saint Clare, with the embroidered initials "KA" referring either to the owner or to the doll. Her outfit was not uncommon for nuns at the time, when the Church played a greater part in English life. Although only 15 in (38 cm) tall, her value is increased as a result of both her fine quality and original clothes.

£20,000–25,000

◀ **PEASANT GIRLS**

Precursors of the 19th-century peg dolls, both of these peasant girls are just over 12 in (30 cm) tall. They are more crudely carved and painted than earlier wooden dolls, with homemade-looking panelled silk dresses in unobtrusive tones and plain hairstyles and bonnets. The hands are poorly represented, and the arms are crudely fashioned. The features are rather brightly painted, the mouth too close to the nose. Doll manufacture was increasing and fashion had turned against the over-the-top rococo style in which dresses were so wide it was impossible to walk through a door without turning sideways like a crab. The result is much less spectacular and lowers the value of this pair.

£4,000–6,000

The 19th century marked a vast expansion in the doll trade as other materials replaced the traditional wood. Papier-mâché was widely used as an inexpensive alternative and poured wax and wax-over-composition and wax-over-papier-mâché also proved good substitutes; as did china and parian. These were all leading up to the enormous boom in French doll manufacturing, first with the fashion dolls and then with the French bébés.

Fashion dolls had their origins in the mannequins and figurines of earlier centuries, usually made in wood or leather and circulated throughout the courts of Europe dressed in the latest mode. In the second half of the 19th century, however, bisque-headed dolls with jointed wood or kid bodies were developed in France at the same time as increasing prosperity led to more interest in both clothes and toys. The new bisque-headed dolls were made to look as realistic as possible. Elaborate construction allowed them to adopt numerous poses and their wardrobes were lavish in the extreme. They were outdone only by the birth of the French bébé, pioneered by dollmaker Pierre François Jumeau, who realized that what little girls loved most were little babies. The craze took off with such fervour that in one year alone in the 1880s the firm of Jumeau sold 85,000 bébés. Curiously, it is often very difficult to distinguish between a bébé and a French fashion doll, except for the length of their similarly extravagant dresses. But bébés are certainly now among the most avidly desired of all collectors' dolls.

GRÖDNERTAL DOLLS

St Ulrich in Grödnertal, Austria, was a major centre for wooden dolls in the 19th century, along with Berchtesgaden, Oberammergau and Sonneberg in Thuringia, Germany. In densely forested regions, whole families were involved in the trade, although the carving and painting tended to be by different craftsmen because of the strict regulations of the guild system.

Grödnertal dolls were originally inexpensive dolls and can be found today for relatively small amounts. They are also known as 'Dutch' peg dolls and penny woodens. The term 'Dutch' probably stems from 'Deutsch' since they were chiefly made in Germany and Austria. 'Penny' reflects their cost, especially towards end of the 19th century, when they were sold at fairs and market stalls.

Features include limbs of carved and turned wood with heads occasionally of china, wax or papier-mâché. The size varies from 1in (2.5 cm) to 24in (61 cm). Hands are spade-like and limbs that show were originally painted white. Faces were gessoed and varnished and are now probably now yellowing with age.

▼ SMALL BUT BEAUTIFUL
This German doll from 1850 is about 6in (15 cm) tall, well carved, painted and wearing her original costume. £350–400

BEWARE
Dryad craft suppliers in London made similar wooden dolls in the 1960s. However, their arm and knee joints were fixed with strips of metal slotted into the wood and held with nails. Their dress was modern but could have been changed. Watch out for pristine period costumes and fresh-looking paintwork.

◀ **QUALITY CURLS**
This fine, large, early doll was made in Germany around 1810–15, and is 19in (48cm) tall. Note the rouged cheeks and carefully painted face, plus the black hair with formalized curls and topknot held in place with a gold band. Some pre-1840 dolls have swivel waists. The hair may be grey and have other adornment, such as a comb, and the shoes may be real instead of painted wood. The dress on this doll is original. £4,500–5,000

▼ **PENNY WOODENS**
This doll from the late-19th century has lost its clothes but none of its appeal. It has crudely painted black hair and its facial features are little more than blobs. The limbs are typically jointed and there is minimal, if any, carving of hands and feet. £50–60

▲ **CHARACTER DOLLS**
Pedlar dolls, usually with baskets or trays of miniature wares and wearing a red cloak, were commonly made in the 19th century. The original baskets are unlikely to have survived and may have been replaced at a later date, but this does not affect the collecting value. All sorts of characters were produced, including clerics, schoolmasters, shopkeepers, fine ladies and gentlemen. £200–£2,000 (depending on the quality of the wares)

PAPIER-MÂCHÉ DOLLS

Papier-mâché was an inexpensive alternative to wood and lighter for export, especially if only the heads were being sent. The German dollmaker Friedrich Müller reputedly learned how to make papier-mâché from a French soldier. He then had the substance pressed into shape by moulds instead of making the dolls individually, so that production was almost mechanical and costs reduced. Thus the Sonneberg doll industry was founded.

Papier-mâché dolls are rarely marked. Their naïve features are similar to those of wooden dolls, with moulded and painted black hair, painted eyes and single-line eyebrows. However, the limbs, either wooden or kid attached to a kid body, are not usually jointed. Joining points may be covered with a paper band, usually pink. The head and shoulders are all one with a deep yoke for gluing to the body. Flesh tones vary between pinkish and yellowish. Hands are spoon-shaped with only a separate thumb.

▶ **BIEDERMEIER DOLL**
This dolls is so named because it dates from the Biedermeier period (1815–48) in Germany. Sometimes known as milliners' models and the precursors to the French fashion dolls, these are the most sought-after nineteenth-century papier-mâché dolls. Hairstyles could be created more successfully in papier-mâché than in wood: this doll has an elaborate bun. She also has a narrow waist and wide hips suitable for the fashions of the period. The head and shoulders are made together. £800–1,000

▲ **DATING CLUES**
Elaborate hairstyles, high-waisted dresses, long necks and thin faces, attributes displayed by the doll on the right, are from the 1820s and 1830s. After this date, as can be seen in the dolls centre and left, the waists are lower and necks may be shorter. The hairstyles are also less complex and the faces are chubbier and more childlike. The middle doll is 17 in (43 cm) tall. £600–1,000 each

FRENCH DOLLS
Some German heads were exported to France. French bodies were mostly made from pink kid with one-piece limbs and a V-shaped central seam on the lower torso. Some have hip and knee gussets and separately stitched fingers.

◄ **GERMAN DOLLS**
These dolls from about
1840 are about 19 in
(48 cm) tall and have
centre-parted, black
moulded hair, painted
eyes, single-line
eyebrows, kid bodies
and wooden lower
limbs with spoon-
shaped hands.
From left to right:
£600–800 and
£500–700

◄ **GERMAN DOLL**
This typical German
doll of about 1840 is
19 in (48 cm) tall, has
moulded and painted
black hair, painted
eyes and single-line
eyebrows. The lower
limbs are wooden,
attached to a kid body.
Note the spoon-shaped
hands with a separate
thumb. £800–1,200

BEWARE
Papier-mâché is difficult to restore,
so the condition is vital. Heads
often crack and any such defect
will reduce value. Arms are usually
straight, so if they are made of
composition and wire to allow
them to bend, it could be they
are of a later date.

► **FRENCH DOLL**
This large, early
French fashion doll
dates from 1840 and
measures about 30 in
(76 cm) tall. She has
black, pupil-less eyes,
pierced nostrils and
painted eyes. With
open-mouthed dolls
of this type, bamboo
was used for the teeth.
£500–700

POURED-WAX DOLLS

Wax dolls undoubtedly evolved from the funeral effigies and religious figures that were produced throughout Europe during the Middle Ages. Wax could be made to resemble the colour of human skin very closely if it were tinted and mixed with substances such as animal fat and turpentine. But, as wax was expensive, only wealthy parents could afford wax dolls for their children.

Wax dolls were made by two different methods. Dolls with solid carved wax heads, known as pressed-wax dolls, were made until 1840. Due to cost, they usually had a small head, with glass bead eyes, stylized features, solid wax arms and legs, a real hair wig and unseparated fingers and toes. Poured-wax dolls were similarly expensive, although the head and limbs were only shells. They were formed by pouring molten wax into a mould, allowing an outer crust to harden, draining off the excess and repeating the process until the required thickness was achieved. Several Italian families based in London dominated the industry, which escalated after they began to make the first true baby dolls – modelled specifically on Queen Victoria's children.

◀ SEWN HAIR
This doll was made in 1880 and is still wearing the original dress. Its body is cloth and its limbs are made of poured wax. The hair has been inserted on the hairline using a needle. The head is turned slightly to the left and the doll is 20 in (51 cm) tall.
£400–450

BEWARE
It is sometimes difficult to check for repairs on a wax doll because the clothes may be sewn on and there is no fastening. Very pale wax colour may show light damage. The worst damage to watch for is malformation of limbs and extremities due to excessive heat – perhaps from direct sun or central heating. While cracks are easy to restore, malformation is not and will detract as much as one-half of the value.

▶ ITALIAN MAKERS
This award-winning 1850 Montanari doll was modelled on a royal prince and, unusually, is signed. Two Italian families dominated the manufacture of wax dolls. Henry Pierotti, whose father was from northern Italy, supposedly invented the first Royal Model Babies. The dolls often had a turned head and a calico, machine-stitched body. Augusta Montanari, the Pierottis' biggest rival and the makers of this doll, tended to give her dolls a petulant expression, hand-stitched linen bodies and elaborate costumes. Dolls are frequently described as Pierotti-type and Montanari-type, since few are marked.
£3,000–4,000

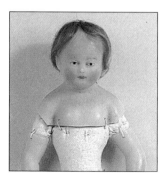

▶ **JOHN EDWARDS**
English dollmaker John
Edwards established his factory
in 1868. He reputedly produced
up to 20,000 wax dolls a
week in 1871, varying from
the inexpensive to commissions
for Queen Victoria. The dolls
were generally unmarked.
An 'E' has been found on an
Edwards doll's shoe, but many
still remain unidentified.
His rare crying baby doll,
almost 20 in (51 cm) tall,
has a very characteristically
pale skin. See also the
particularly detailed modelling.
Note that the doll's value is
increased by its having
belonged to the major
collector Kay Desmonde.
£4,000–6,000

◀ **PEDLAR DOLLS**
Although pedlar dolls are often
wooden, they may also be
of poured wax, as in the case of
this particularly early example
made in England in 1835.
The pedlar is 10 in (25 cm) tall
and her wares (including three
tiny Grödnertal dolls) were
according to a note found on
the table and handwritten by
the dollmaker E. Mabyn. These
were renovated in 1873.
£4,000–6,000

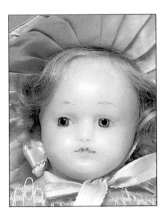

◀ ▶ **PRINCESS ALICE**
Madame Montanari was
renowned for the quality of
her dolls' costumes. This doll is
believed to represent Princess
Alice, third child of Queen
Victoria. She is dressed in an
extremely fine silk dress and
satin-lined bonnet. According
to a note kept with the doll,
she was "modelled by a lady
conversant with the Court".
18-in tall, c.1850. £4,000–6,000

WAX-OVER-COMPOSITION & PAPIER-MÂCHÉ DOLLS

Wax-over-composition and also wax-over-papier-mâché dolls were developed as cheaper alternatives to poured-wax dolls, and are still relatively inexpensive. Wax-over-composition is produced by coating a ready-painted com-position or papier-mâché doll with a layer of molten wax. They were mass-produced in Britain, France and Germany in the 19th century. The three types are known as slit heads, pumpkin heads and wax-overs.

◀ SLIT-HEADS
Slit-head dolls, also known as 'Crazy Alices' were made in England from 1830 onwards. They have a distinctive slit in the crown, into which hair was inserted in a block – a fast and inexpensive process. In common with wooden dolls, faces were crudely modelled, but the wax gave a softer appearance. Most have pupil-less glass eyes and fabric bodies with kid forearms. This 18 in- (46 cm-) tall doll dates from 1845 and has suffered some crazing, but it is still attractive, wearing an original outfit and proving that faded elegance is better than restoration. £300–400

BEWARE
Damage to the heads of later dolls seriously reduces their worth. Wax-over dolls of all types are very susceptible to crazing – becoming covered in a network of fine cracks. This is as a result of the expansion and contraction (which occurs during changes in temperature) of the different materials from which they are made. However, colourful and elaborate original costumes increase their value considerably.

▲ PUMPKIN-HEADS
Made in England and Germany c.1860, pumpkin-heads – so-called because of their large, hollow, moulded heads that were painted after being dipped in wax – gradually replaced slit-heads. They usually have moulded hair, and dolls which have real hair and moulded bonnets, known as a bonnet-heads, are especially desirable. £150–200

▼ ▶ REALISM
Dolls made late in the century
appear more realistic. Dark hair
was rarer than blonde. This doll
was made in France and has
blue, paperweight glass eyes –
like those on highly fashionable
but more expensive bisque dolls.
German examples have flatter,
spun-glass eyes. £300–400

▼ WAX-OVERS
Dolls made of wax-over-
composition, but of neither slit
head nor pumpkin-head type,
were made in the 1870s in
Germany and France. They
often appear similar to china
and parian dolls of the same
period. £200–500 depending
on the original clothes.

**WHAT TO
LOOK FOR**
● Slit-head dolls should
have a reasonable
abundance of
remaining hair.
● With pumpkin-
head dolls, the more
elaborate the
hairstyle and
moulded bonnet,
the better.

◀ CHRISTMAS FAIRIES
Fairy dolls were made as
inexpensive decorations for
Christmas trees, a fashion
introduced by Prince Albert
in the second half of the 19th
century. Many have survived
in good condition, despite the
danger from candles, as they are
brought out only once a year.
A deep-pink flesh colour is a
distinctive feature of later dolls.
£100–150

CHINA DOLLS

The secret of making porcelain, long known to the Chinese, was first discovered in Europe in 1709 by a German alchemist working for Meissen. Porcelain factories were established in Thuringia, Germany, which was already a doll-making centre and china dolls were an obvious progression. Their shoulder-heads were made from glazed, hard-paste porcelain and attached to the rest of the body by glue, nails or stitches through specially made holes.

From the 1840s to the end of the century these dolls were produced in huge numbers.

Many famous porcelain factories including Royal Copenhagen, Meissen and Königliche Porzellan Manufaktur (KPM) made dolls, but they were rarely marked except by KPM. German dolls had their features painted on and fired. Fewer French dolls were made and they were more refined, sometimes with swivel heads, glass eyes and real hair.

▶ **EMPRESS EUGENIE**
Dolls with dark-brown rather than black hair in elaborate, deeply moulded styles adorned with lustre ornaments are the most sought-after by collectors. This 20 in (51 cm) German doll has black, finely painted hair, feathered at the sides and arranged in ringlets, and a gold-painted snood and tassels. She has red painted lines on her eyelids and is wearing an original silk dress. Empress Eugenie, as this type of doll is called, was modelled on the wife of Napoleon III and is one of the best examples of German china doll manufacture. China dolls modelled on the young Queen Victoria were also popular. £1,000–1,500

BEWARE

If bodies and clothes have been replaced, the doll's value is reduced. Dolls made towards the end of the century are less desirable. Known as 'lowbrows' in contrast with earlier 'highbrows', their hair tends to be lower on the forehead, black (sometimes blonde), short and centre-parted with curls around the back and sides.

WHAT TO LOOK FOR

● An oddly shaped cotton body may indicate that the doll is home-made, as china heads could be bought separately.
● Commercial manufacturers used a wide range of body materials but generally painted legs with black boots and fancy garters.
● Before 1860, all shoes were flat.

▶ IDENTIFICATION

An 1890 German doll, she has a typical white face with red cheeks, black hair and blue eyes. Her red, rosebud mouth indicates that she is German. Early dolls are the most elegant, with a red line on the eyelid and possibly a pink-tinted face. Some particularly delicate examples made between 1845 and 1860, known as 'Biedermeier chinas', have a bald head with a black spot on top covered by a curled plait of real hair. Less common French dolls, which were made alongside French fashion dolls, have closed, smiling mouths – different from those of their German contemporaries. £300–400

▲▶ MOTSCHMANN-TYPE

These dolls are named after a papier-mâché doll with a voice-box, marked Charles Motschmann and dated 1857, which was found in a German museum. They have a porcelain shoulder-head and floating limbs connected by a loose fabric midriff, which may conceal a bellows voice-box operated by a pull string. This one was made in Germany c.1850 and has black moulded hair held with an Alice band, a rare swivel neck, original costume and a china and cloth body containing a squeaker. £300–400

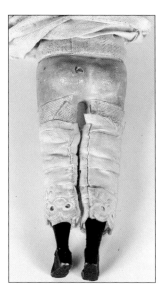

PARIAN DOLLS

Parian dolls were made chiefly between 1870 and the end of the 19th century using the same porcelain paste as was employed for chinas, but the paste was left unglazed to give a matt finish. The difference between parian and bisque is that bisque is tinted with a coloured pigment while parian is left untinted and as a result the dolls have a white marble-like skin tone. Parian was a trade name originally used by the English porcelain firm Copeland & Garrett and stems from the island of Paros in Greece which is famous for its white marble. Most of these dolls, however, were made in Germany.

Due to their fragility, parian dolls are relatively rare. Some restoration or unrestored damage is acceptable and even heads without bodies are worth collecting.

▶ **SUGAR SWEET**
Parian dolls tend to have a very sugary appearance due to the paste used. This is frequently emphasized by fancy garments with lace and frills, as in this 20 in (51 cm) German doll from 1890. Note the rather chubby face and the hairstyle which is highly fashionable for the time and helps to date the doll. £300–400

▶ **CHILDREN**
Parian child dolls, like this 1870 example, are rare and consequently their value is enhanced. Towards the end of the century faces became generally more rounded and childlike with short necks and simple hairstyles set low on the forehead. This doll has glass eyes. Painted eyes were more common. £500–700

WHAT TO LOOK FOR
• Dolls were often moulded with details of jewellery or clothing which were painted and then fired along with the facial details.
• Many parian dolls have pierced ears.
• End-of-the-century dolls may have moulded bonnets.

GERMAN PARIAN

THIS TYPICAL EXAMPLE OF
GOOD GERMAN PARIAN
WAS MADE IN 1890.
UNFORTUNATELY, MAKERS'
MARKS ARE RARE: IF A DOLL
HAS ONE IT WILL PROBABLY BE
ON THE BACK OF THE NECK.
£600–800

Blonde hair is usual: the
best dolls have elaborate
styles. Some have
moulded ornaments or
applied flowers.

Smiles are rare: this doll
has the very typical
closed mouth.

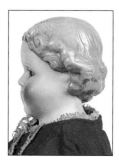

▲ This hairstyle
became popular in
the mid-1880s

Bisque lower limbs
were attached to the
stuffed body, which
had a narrow waist
and wide hips.

The clothes are original,
even including the hat,
which is usually the first
item to be lost.

Moulded and painted
gold lustre boots (see
right) added style.

FRENCH FASHION DOLLS I: JUMEAU & MADAME ROHMER

Fashion dolls, or 'Parisiennes', were produced between 1860–90. Heads (and sometimes also limbs) were bisque and the dolls represented the fashionable ladies of the period who changed into many different dresses a day. They evolved from mannequin figurines and fashion-house 'Pandoras'. These display models, a head and torso up to 36in (90cm) tall on a collapsible stand, were exported as Paris became the fashion capital of the world. Bodies were in various styles and materials.

and construction was elaborate to allow the dolls to adopt the most natural poses. Their complexion was realistically tinted and their glass eyes and real-hair wigs added to their naturalistic appearance. Adult dolls are easily distinguishable from bébés by their thin waist. Dolls with swivel necks are worth double those with rigid necks. Fashion dolls are mostly attributed by type since few were marked and prices remain around the 1988 level after too many appeared on the market.

WHAT TO LOOK FOR

● Rohmer dolls tend to have delicately detailed, rounded faces.
● The most valuable come with their original wardrobe contained in a trunk, complete with everything down to fur muff and parasol.
● Glass eyes are rarer than painted eyes.
● Jumeau eyes tend to have quite a soulful, emotional expression.

▶ **SYMBOL OF AFFLUENCE**
Expensive fashion dolls were bought for children as a symbol of their parents' wealth and status. They also helped a young girl to develop a fashion-sense and improve her sewing skills by adding clothes to a doll's large wardrobe, which was essential. This 1878 Jumeau swivel-head doll, 20in (51cm) tall, has her original box.

Identification of a doll's original clothes can be difficult, since even the original owner may have added to her outfits from time to time. The best guide is usually to examine the fit.
£7,000–8,000

BEWARE
Firing lines and other porcelain defects may reduce a doll's value. Raised pink spots are not uncommon, but much may depend on where the problem is and if the defect makes the doll less attractive. Wire inside the kid body, allowing limbs to move, may create rust marks.

▶ **JUMEAU**

The firm of Jumeau (1842–99) was at the forefront of the French doll industry and its dolls are the ultimate collectable. Pierre Jumeau was the founder, eventually handing over to his youngest son Emile in 1875. Jumeau dolls were famous for their elegant clothes, as in this 1875 example, 20 in (51 cm) tall. £4,000–5,000

▲ **IDENTIFICATION**

Look for large almond-shaped eyes that are particularly expressive due to the use of blue spiral glass – the white thread running through the iris giving an impression of depth. This 20 in- (51 cm-) tall 1865 doll has the typical closed mouth and pierced ears. The body should be kid with separate fingers and toes. The name of the shop or maker is occasionally found placed under the kid on the shoulder-plate. £7,000–8,000

▶ **MADAME ROHMER**

Marie Antoinette Léontine Rohmer's company operated only from 1857 to 1880. Her dolls are scarce but they are of very high quality. However, due to the fact that the factory produced a variety of heads on differing body types, identification is extremely difficult. These two early Rohmer dolls are both 14 in (36 cm) tall, but their values differ considerably because the doll on the left has glass eyes and a swivel head, whereas the other has a rigid neck and painted eyes.

LEFT £7,000–8,000
RIGHT £3,000–4,000

FRENCH FASHION DOLLS II: GAULTIER & BRU JEUNE

Gaultier and Bru Jeune were two of the most important 19th-century firms. François Gaultier (1860–99), 'Gaultier' until 1875, made bisque-headed dolls on a variety of bodies: gusseted kid, gutta-percha (latex) and articulated wood or metal padded with kapok and covered with stockinette. The company also made heads for other dollmakers. Gesland, a French doll repairs and spare parts firm, used Gaultier heads for bodies dressed in regional costume, popular souvenirs among European tourists in the 1880s. Hands and legs were bisque and bodies usually labelled.

Bru Jeune et Cie (later Bru Jeune), which was established in 1866 by Léon Casimir Bru in Rue St Denis, Paris, made bisque-headed dolls using various types of body until 1883. Initially, the heads were supplied by other firms, such as Barrois and Jumeau, whose dolls have many similarities. Later, Bru began to experiment with smiling dolls and dolls that could laugh and cry.

◀ **ACCENTUATED MEASUREMENTS**
Fashion dolls can be identified and dated generally by the shape of their body. This late 19th-century Gaultier doll has a typically narrow waist and wide shoulders and hips. The shape was ideal for its original bustled dress. £2,000–3,000

▶ **CHARACTERISTICS**
A typical 1870 Gaultier doll measures an average height of 23 in (58 cm). This example has large, piercing eyes, a closed mouth, real hair over a cork pate and a swivel neck. Hats were especially important to achieve the total Parisienne-chic look. £2,000–3,000

▲ **GAULTIER**
This 1875 Gaultier doll is particularly large at 27 in (69 cm). The body is made out of gusseted kid. It has separately stitched fingers and toes, which are more desirable than 'mitten' hands and feet which are stitched in one block. £4,000–5,000

BEWARE

Gaultier was an exception in marking most of its fashion dolls on the shoulder and/or back of the crown of the head. It is important when checking a doll to be sure that the head and body belong together. Many Gaultier heads were sold for use by other firms who attached their own bodies. These dolls would not be marked on the bisque except for maybe a number denoting the size. The Gaultier fashion doll and bébé are recognizable mainly by the slightly smiling mouths and well-defined upper lips.

▼ SMILING DOLLS

In 1873, Bru registered a smiling doll with a swivel head on a bisque shoulder-plate, purportedly modelled (like others) on the Empress Eugenie, wife of Napoleon III and said to be the most beautiful woman in France. The bodies are all kid or kid with wooden or bisque arms and occasionally wooden articulated arms. This typical doll is dated 1875 and is 25 in (64 cm) tall. £12,000–15,000

◀ TWO-FACED DOLLS

Two-faced dolls which have a waking and a sleeping face were patented in 1868 as a development of the laughing and crying dolls made by Bru. The swivel head is rotated to reveal the alternative face. £6,000–8,000

WHAT TO LOOK FOR

● Early Bru dolls may be marked "Depose" or "Bru Jne et Cie" or "BJ".
● Later dolls may have only letters relating to size.

BRU Jⁿᵉ et Cⁱᵉ Nᵒ 1

DEPOSE

BÉBÉ BRU
Nᵒ 1

FRENCH FASHION DOLLS III

Doll accessories were so important that there was a whole range of accessory manufacturers working in the Passage Choiseul area of Paris – including doll milliners, cobblers, corset-makers and glove-makers. Specialist shops also sold miniature fans, jewellery, underwear and a host of other minute objects, while various publications such as *La Poupée Modèle* advised girls on the latest doll fashions and included patterns for making clothes at home. Fashion dolls frequently came equipped with trunks full of other outfits and accessories. If the trunks and their contents are still with the doll, they add hugely to its value.

▶ **WARDROBES**

Dolls' wardrobes sometimes turn up for sale separately, so if you have a doll without its original clothes it may be worth hunting for period replacements. A relatively small outlay on the right garments can greatly increase a doll's value. This 16 in (41 cm) doll made in 1870 by Rohmer is displayed here with an extraordinary range of clothes and accessories which should equip her for every occasion. £6,000–8,000

> **BEWARE**
> Trunks of tiny clothes need special care. Watch out for moths and layer with acid-free tissue (see pages 30–31).

◀ **SCHMITT & FILS**

The makers of this doll, Schmitt of Paris (1863–91), were originally children's toymakers. But in 1877 sons Maurice and Charles were granted a patent for decorating porcelain shoulder-heads by a method that allowed any shade to be given to a bisque head. They later added a layer of wax, supposedly to improve the doll's appearance and make it more durable. From 1885 Schmitt developed eye movement in dolls. This doll was made about 1880 and has a long face. There are many different "looks" to Schmitt dolls, starting with the early round faces and changing expressions. The paler, long-faced ones are more sought-after as they look more appealing. Their bodies are usually stamped with a shield and two hammers. The limbs are shaped and their heels are more pronounced than with other dolls. £4,000–6,000

MYSTERY WOMAN

EXACT IDENTIFICATION OF MANUFACTURER OR ORIGIN IS NOT VITAL. DESPITE THE LACK OF ANY SPECIFIC MARK THIS 1860 DOLL IS VALUABLE. SHE IS 18 IN (46 CM) TALL, OF OBVIOUS QUALITY AND HER IMPORTANCE IS INCREASED BY HAVING BEEN IN THE BODMER COLLECTION (SEE PAGE 84). FEW DOLLS BEAR A MAKER'S MARK, BUT MANY CAN BE ATTRIBUTED BY THEIR CHARACTERISTICS. THOSE OF THIS DOLL COULD POINT TO SEVERAL OF THE TOP FRENCH FIRMS – BUT HER IDENTITY REMAINS A PUZZLE. £30,000–40,000

The eyes are fixed blue glass.

The white mohair wig is over a cork pate.

Black eyeliner, a shading line and red inner dots emphasize upper lid. Lashes are finely painted.

The smiling mouth is closed.

The brows are well feathered.

She has a slight double chin and a swivel head.

The wooden body is leather covered and has disc joints at hip and knee. She wears muslin underwear.

The arms are bisque.

The sky-blue, ribbed-silk coat with cut-silk tassles and satin edging is original.

Hidden under the coat are maroon leather lace-up heeled boots.

The detail on the cream silk dress matches the shorter coat.

FRENCH BÉBÉS I: JUMEAU

Until the 19th century, dolls were modelled and dressed as adults. However, after the London dollmaker Henry Pierotti created his Royal Model Babies representing the children of Queen Victoria, it was then realized that children prefer to play with dolls that more resemble themselves.

In 1855, leading Paris dollmaker Pierre François Jumeau was the first off the mark to make a bébé, as this type of doll became known. Rival firms quickly copied him as demand grew from wealthy families.

The heyday of the bébé, along with the French fashion doll, occurred between the 1860s and 1890s, when France replaced Germany as the world's top doll manufacturer. Bébés took the form of idealized young girls,

with bisque heads, real hair, either wool or mohair wigs, large (usually glass) eyes and delicately painted facial details. Their bodies were jointed, and made in varying materials – but with noticeably chubby limbs and also a gently rounded stomach. At first their mouths were closed and their wrists were fixed. The use of articulated wrists and open mouths on bébés came later.

Today, bébés are the most popular type of doll with collectors. Prices range from just a few hundred to many thousands of pounds, depending on maker, condition, quality and certain vital details. The earlier dolls with pale, flawless bisque heads are considered to be the most valuable, especially if they have their original, fashionable clothes.

▶ **JUMEAU**
This leading French doll firm and bébé pioneer introduced portrait bébés, supposedly modelled on real children, in 1870. Emile Jumeau took over the company in 1875 and maximized his father's success. From this date onwards, dolls bearing his mark are referred to as E.J.s. This is an 11in- (28 cm-) tall portrait Jumeau dated 1870. £7,000–8,000

◀ **JUMEAU CHARACTERISTICS**
Especially elaborate dress and accessories, as shown in this E.J. doll, with original silk and lace dress and bonnet, were very popular. Bébés were given blue eyes with long lashes then highlighted with black eyeliner. The bee motif was common on shoes (not shown in picture). Most early dolls have a Jumeau mark on the head, then on the body, after Jumeau won a gold medal at the 1878 Paris Exposition Universelle. The rarest is marked with an "A". £10,000–12,000

▶ **TWO-FACED DOLLS**
Crying and laughing dolls are
rare. The head is turned to
reveal one face or the other by
operating a knob in the top of
the hair. The bisque tends to be
rather pink. £6,000–8,000

◀ **JUMEAU TRISTE**
The Jumeau Triste, or long-
faced bébé, is especially sought
after. Despite body repainting,
plain dress and a missing shoe,
this 1875 doll is very valuable,
partly because of her unusually
large size. She is nearly 32 in
(81 cm) tall. £15,000–18,000

◀ **VLADIMIR**
A rare boy bébé,
27 in (69 cm) tall,
this doll was given
to Miss Ellen West,
who was governess
to the children of the
Duke and Duchess of
Edinburgh as a leaving
present in 1900. He
is wearing the smart
sailor uniform of the
Imperial Russian Navy,
the cap bearing the
title in Cyrillic of the
Yacht Roxana. The
doll was probably
a commission by a
relative of the children
and owner of the
yacht, Duke George
of Leuchtenberg.
This romantic tale
is only conjecture
as there is no firm
documentation to
confirm the story,
hence the value of
the doll is relatively
low. Note how the
gender of the doll
is conveyed by the
choice of costume
rather than by using
any variation in
the doll's facial
characteristics.
£4,000–6,000

FRENCH BÉBÉS II: BRU JEUNE

Léon Casimir Bru established Bru Jeune et Cie in 1866. He produced innovative bébés: one patented as a "Bru Téteur" in 1879 could suck from a bottle and 'Bébé Gourmand' could be fed morsels of food which were then carried through a tube in the hollow body to an opening in the foot. Bru was Jumeau's biggest rival until 1899, when both joined an association with other dollmakers to fight the German competition. Bru Jeune was sold in

1883 to Henri Chevrot, although he retained the name and label. He concentrated on top-quality dolls for several years and experimented with rubber and swimming dolls.

Towards the end of the 1880s a decline began, with competition increasing from Germany, and Bru was taken over by Chevrot's friend Paul Eugène Girard. Using the mark "Bru Jne R", Girard went in for novel, less expensive dolls.

WHAT TO LOOK FOR
- Before 1880, arms were on a wire armature and had bisque forearms.
- From 1880, arms became articulated, with upper arms made from wood covered in kid and a ball joint at the elbow.
- From the early 1880s, heads were attached by a metal wing-nut and spring.

▼ BRU TÉTEUR
This 1883 doll is a Bru Téteur, which could suck from a bottle. A rubber bulb in the head was squeezed manually at first, then by pressing an external ivory knob and finally by turning a wing-nut to exert pressure.
£4,000–5,000

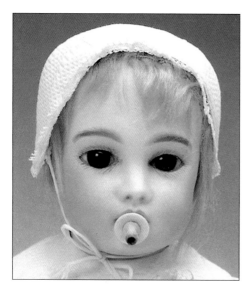

▲ BRU JEUNE CHARACTERISTICS
This bébé's wooden lower legs indicate an early example. A "BRU Jne" stamp is likely, as in this case, on the head and shoulders; a stamp may also be found on original shoes, and a brown and beige paper label on the body. This large 1880 doll, almost 36 in (91 cm) tall, has the remains of a label on the chest. The dress can make a huge difference to value.
£20,000–25,000

▶ **CIRCLE AND DOT DOLLS**
These dolls are so-called because of the circle and dot mark found on the back of the head, possibly caused during moulding. Especially fine dolls made by Bru are rare today. They usually have a distinctive open/closed mouth with the very slightest simulation of teeth. This one, dated 1875, has a later hat, but the value is high.
£15,000–16,000

▼ **NOVELTIES**
This 1895 Girard doll with a composition and wood body can walk, talk and blow kisses. The voice-box is activated by the legs moving, and cries "Mama". The jointed right arm is worked to blow kisses by a pull string from the waist. The painting on the face is less refined than earlier Bru bébés. The open mouth with upper teeth and the heavy, dark feather eyebrows are also typical of Girard.
£3,000–4,000

◀ **ETHNIC DOLLS**
In 1883, Bru began producing Oriental and black dolls like the one pictured, with fired red lips. They are extremely rare, and there are many fakes. Other firms, including Gaultier, Jumeau and Simon & Halbig, produced mulatto and Negro dolls for the 1878 and 1889 Paris Exhibitions showing various characteristics of natives from French colonies. The fakes have either lips painted red *after* firing or lips which are the same brownish colour as the face tint.
£25,000–30,000

FRENCH BÉBÉS III: STEINER

Steiner was a Paris firm set up in 1855 by clockmaker Jules Nicholas Steiner, who first created walking, talking dolls. The best period for his dolls is the 1880s when he was working with J. Bourgoin, to whom he rented his factory. The company was taken over in 1890 by Lafosse, and quality gradually declined.

The Motschmann type of doll, with a bisque shoulder-head and floating limbs attached to a loose fabric midriff incorporating a voice-box (see page 107), was also made by Steiner. The dolls may not be marked – but look out for the tell-tale signs of narrow, almond-shaped eyes and delicate eyebrows.

▶ CHARACTERISTICS
Early bébés have stubby hands and, as with this 1870 doll, jointed papier-mâché bodies which are coloured purple beneath the flesh paint. The mouth is positioned rather close to the nose. Later Steiners with slender fingers also have well-defined big toes. The finest dolls may be stamped by both Steiner and Bourgoin. This bébé, nearly 20 in (51 cm) tall, is cracked on the temple which slightly reduces its value. £2,000–3,000

▲ EARLY DESIGN
This doll's full title was an autoperipatetikos crying doll. The cardboard conical skirt under her original blue chintz dress hides bellows and a stop-start mechanism which causes the wheels in the wooden base to rotate and the doll to 'walk'. The design was used widely through the early period. This 1865 doll has a typical open mouth with two rows of teeth and also fixed glass eyes. £1,000–1,500

BEWARE
Steiner bébé faces were painted by different artists so details vary. As company records were incomplete, exact dating is difficult. Management also changed often so there are many different Steiner marks. Some mechanical dolls are marked only on the mechanism; some heads are marked "J. Steiner" or "Ste" until in 1889 a trademark was registered showing a baby holding a flag. This was used as a body stamp.

▲ STEINER MARK

This blue ink stamp on the left hip indicates a Bébé Le Parisien Médaille D'Or Paris. This means it was made in 1889 when Steiner won the medal in Paris. The body is fully jointed except for the wrists, and the head is marked "Steiner Bté S.G.D.G. Bté" meaning it is patented ("Bté" stands for *breveté* or patent) but without government guarantee (S.G.D.G. stands for *Sans Guarantie Du Gouvernement*) of the patent.

▶ BÉBÉ PREMIER PAS

The wind-up mechanism of this doll, a type patented in 1890, makes it walk while its hand is held. The key is of course normally covered by clothing. The bisque head is of inferior material and poorly painted, suggesting it is a very late model. Earlier examples, which command much higher prices, had detailed painting and expressive eyes. The body is jointed wood and composition. £3,000–4,000

▼ WIRE-EYED DOLLS

These dolls are known as 'wire-eyed' because of the wire lever at the side of the head that opened and closed the eyes. This doll was made in 1880 when Bourgoin was running the factory but Steiner was still advising. £5,000–6,000

▲ GESLAND LABEL

The Gesland label was used from the turn of the century for bébés with German heads on Steiner bodies. The dolls were assembled by the doll repair and spare parts firm, the Gesland Co, which operated from 1860 to 1915 and had interests in making French regional-costume dolls.

FRENCH BÉBÉS IV: SCHMITT & A.T.

Schmitt produced bisque and bisque-headed bébés at Nogent-sur-Marne in France from 1863–91. Besides developing moving eyes, the company became famous for an 'indestructible' Bébé Schmitt, which was exported as well as being sold in France from 1879 onwards, and is now highly collectable. The firm of A. Thuillier, known as A.T., operated in Paris from 1875 to 1890. Dolls were sold dressed and undressed with kid, composition and papier-mâché jointed bodies. A.T. sometimes used bodies and heads made by other dollmakers such as Steiner and Gaultier. The dolls command very high prices today because of their rarity. Both firms were renowned for the beauty of their dolls.

▶ **SCHMITT CHARACTERISTICS**
Schmitt dolls such as this typically have a body including eight ball-joints. It is extra long and has slender feet along with a flat bottom to the torso. Schmitt's trademark of crossed hammers within a shield should appear on both head and body. This 1885 doll has fixed glass eyes, an open/closed mouth, showing white between the lips, and real hair. Straight rather than jointed wrists signify an early date. The body has particularly well-formed upper arms and the heels are usually more pronounced. The shield mark is usually in black and is stamped under the bottom.
£7,000–9,000

◀ **A.T. CHARACTERISTICS**
Paperweight eyes with pink shading behind are a distinguishing characteristic of A.T. dolls. Some bébés have open mouths with two rows of teeth. This 1880 bébé has a papier-mâché jointed body and an exquisite head with a closed mouth, fixed blue-glass eyes and a lovely blonde, real hair wig.
£25,000–30,000

> **BEWARE**
> Do not confuse Schmitt with later Franz Schmidt German dolls, which carry a similar trademark. This is confusing as exported Schmitt dolls were sometimes referred to as Schmidt.

▶ **RIGHT HEAD,
WRONG BODY**

A rare, small-sized 1880 boy doll, less than 11 in (28 cm) tall has a Schmitt bisque head with crossed hammer mark, fixed eyes and a closed mouth. However, the body is made by Jumeau and bears a Médaille D'Or Paris stamp. Although Schmitt did often use Jumeau bodies, purist collectors will now buy heads only on the Schmitt body. £6,000–8000

WHAT TO LOOK FOR

- Check for Schmitt or A.T. marks.
- Are head and body both by the same factory?
- Does the doll represent the ideal little girl or boy?
- Is everything about the doll exquisite?
- The clothes are high-fashion including gloves, bonnets and shoes
- The best materials (silks and satins) are used on the clothes.

▶ **TOP DOLL**

This was the most expensive bébé in the sale when auctioned at Sotheby's in 1992 for £29,000. She is almost 20 in (51 cm) tall, dated 1875, and bears the impressed "A.T." mark. She has fixed blue-glass paperweight eyes, pierced ears and a blonde mohair wig over a cork pate. The body is gusseted kid. She has bisque forearms and is wearing an original blue ribbed-silk dress with cream-lace front panels. Value has risen substantially, chiefly due to rarity. £40,000–50,000

▲ **A.T. CHARMER**

This A.T. doll is 16 in (41 cm) tall. Her original pink dress is trimmed with silk and black ribbon. She has a jointed papier-mâché body, blue paperweight eyes and real auburn hair. £30,000–40,000

FRENCH BÉBÉS V:
OTHER FRENCH MAKERS

Dollmaking became a major industry in France in the latter part of the 19th century and small firms sprang up everywhere, especially in porcelain-making areas such as Limoges. Toy firms also jumped on the bandwagon, buying heads and bodies from other makers, and some dolls were sold unfinished to be completed at home. So, besides the major names there are a multitude of other variations. Quality varies equally widely. For a doll from a lesser-known factory to be considered valuable it must be in good condition, well made and attractive. Few match up to the top French names and indeed any mystery doll that does so will probably turn out to be by a leading manufacturer.

◀ GAULTIER
These bébés, noted for the size and quality of their fixed glass paperweight or bulbous eyes, often had small pointed chins, pierced ears and chubby cheeks. Pre-1885 lightly arched eyebrows are thin; later they are dark and glossy. This 36 in- (91 cm-) doll has a jointed wood and composition body. Closed mouth and size both increase the value. £7,000–8,000

▼ ROHMER
This 20 in- (51 cm-) rare Rohmer child doll was made in 1860, three years after the company was founded. She has a flange, swivel neck (in fact patented by Madame Huret in 1858) to allow the head to turn from side to side on a bisque shoulder-plate, and gusseted kid body with bisque forearms. She bears a green oval stamp on the abdomen. £4,000–5,000

◀ MAISON HURET
This small family firm at Montmartre, Paris (1850–1920) was renowned for its jointed dolls and invented the socket swivel neck. Bébés were usually unmarked although some carry Paris Exhibition stamps. A double chin, closed mouth and painted eyes indicate a very early bébé. £6,000–8,000

▶ **LIMOGES**

Several Limoges porcelain factories made dolls' heads and whole dolls between 1897 and 1925. Their quality is generally poor, and the colouring of some is rather too pink. This doll has pierced ears, sleep eyes and Limoges moulded teeth. The example shown here was perhaps made as late as 1910. £300–400

▼ **RABERY & DELPHIEU**

The firm was granted a patent for dolls in 1856 and introduced talkers in 1890. It purchased heads and arms from Gaultier and made assorted versions with swivel or stationary heads and pink or white kid, composition or wood bodies. This example is impressed "R.3.D" and has fixed brown glass eyes as well as a jointed composition body. She appears rather boss-eyed. This is a type that appears regularly on the market and is thus more affordable. £4,000–5,000

▲ **CONTROVERSY**

A Jumeau director called Danel quit amid much acrimony in 1889 to found his own factory with a partner, Guepratte, at Montreuil-sous-Bois. Jumeau won a lawsuit against Danel for enticing Jumeau workers to join him, borrowing moulds and other equipment and taking heads and bodies. This large bébé (36in/91cm) with applied ears and a Jumeau body was probably made just as Danel was leaving Jumeau. The doll is stamped with the 'Paris Bébé' mark registered by Danel & Cie, who used a picture of the Eiffel Tower as their trademark. The firm began to specialize in black dolls before being taken over by Jumeau again in 1896. This example is valuable due to both its size and rarity. £10,000–15,000

FRENCH BÉBÉS VI: S.F.B.J.

Société Française de Fabrication de Bébés et Jouets (1899–1950) had its main period before 1930. Usually known as S.F.B.J., it was an association of major French dollmakers who feared the intrusion of German manufacturers and teamed up anonymously to form a consortium against the competition. Based at the Jumeau factory, they made boy and girl characters, coloured dolls and bébés, mostly producing bisque-headed bébés on jointed wood and composition bodies. The dolls were generally numbered according to the mould used. Most frequent moulds are numbers 60 and 301, both of which have dolly-type faces. There were also many character faces.

Ironically, despite the intense rivalry, doll parts were sometimes imported from Germany. Most notable were the Simon & Halbig heads used between 1900 and 1914. By 1922 the S.F.B.J. had 2,800 employees and was using 2,000 different models, including black dolls which were especially popular in the French colonies. Many dolls were sold in South America and Australia, but the Americans tended to buy German dolls. In 1925 the S.F.B.J. was running eight factories.

▼ CHILDREN'S FAVOURITE
Made in 1910, this is a good example of a mould No. 60. It has a typical bisque head on a jointed wood and composition body. The doll, which is nearly 24in (61 cm) tall, was made in 1910.
£300–500

▲ CHARACTERS
By 1911, the S.F.B.J. were manufacturing characters to compete with the realistic characters which German factories had begun producing at the beginning of the century. These are much better made than the association's bébés. This one has unusually flirty eyes, more often found on later dolls. The bisque face is both pale and delicately moulded. The jointed wood and composition body has typically elongated fingers.
£800–1,000

◀ BODIES

This is a doll from mould No. 301 with the usual jointed wood and composition body. These dolls are likely to be of slimmer proportions than earlier dolls with high-cut legs. They are distinguishable from their German counterparts by the lack of separate ball joints at the elbow and knee. £400–£600

▼ BOY DOLLS

Two S.F.B.J. character moulds are shown here. The black boy (left) is mould no 227 from 1910 and the boy on the right is mould no 235. His "hair" is flock, which is stuck onto a domed head which has moulded but not coloured hair below. In good condition: £1,500–2,000 and £2,000–3,000 respectively.

FASHION EXPERTS

In 1912, S.F.B.J. advertised that five million dolls a year were being produced at their Vincennes factory alone. These were sent to Paris to be dressed in the latest styles by several hundred women, some fashion-house experts, with prizes offered each year for improvements. The result was stylish dressing, with less attention being paid to the actual doll.

MARKS

"S.F.B.J." was stamped on the back of the head of most dolls from 1905 onwards, along with the mould number. Circular stickers may also be found on the body. Sometimes the actual date was the mould of a particular doll looking like the original Jumeau. Similar to their German counterparts, S.F.B.J. gave incised numbers to different moulds, thereby creating "character moulds".

German dollmakers, whose supremacy had been ousted in the 19th century by French fashion and bébé dolls, retaliated towards the end of the century by producing quality child dolls at lower prices, making them accessible to many more children. By the 1890s, huge numbers of these German bisque girl dolls were flooding the market and the French factories had established the S.F.B.J. (see pages 126–7). However, by the turn of the century demand was growing for more realistic-looking dolls.

Kämmer & Reinhardt were the first to make a character baby, the Kaiser Baby, which looked too ugly to be popular. But lifelike character dolls were produced by Germany's top manufacturers until 1930, most notably J.D. Kestner, Armand Marseille, Simon & Halbig and Gebruder Heubach. Bisque versions of two American cartoon-inspired dolls, Googlies and Kewpies, were made in huge quantities in the 1920s for the United States.

Meanwhile, the creation of the Golliwog also sparked a demand for fabric and rag dolls which had long been traditional to American teddy-bear manufacturers. Steiff were among the leaders, along with Lenci, who made designer dolls. New materials such as celluloid, followed by plastic and vinyl, offered great potential – and America took the lead because of the Second World War. Barbie, the American vinyl doll which was created in 1959, has proved the most successful doll ever made and the rarer Barbies are among the most sought-after dolls in the world.

GERMAN CHARACTER DOLLS I

These are much sought after because of the range of styles and prices. Early Kämmer & Reinhardt and the rarer Simon & Halbig dolls tend to be the most expensive. Kestners and Armand Marseilles are less rare and cheaper. Cost is also influenced by the quality of decoration, body style and condition. Pale bisque is preferred. Over-simplified facial details will reduce value, as will a bent-limb body.

Simon & Halbig were one of Germany's earliest and most prolific bisque head manufacturers, making heads for other German and French companies. The firm first produced shoulder-heads up to 1880 and then socket-heads, with very fine character heads after 1900. Sleeping eyes and real hair eyelashes were introduced on some dolls from 1895 onwards. Almost all heads have a mould number, which is particularly important to notice when collecting these dolls.

▲ HILDA
Character dolls were made by Kestner in the '200' series of marks. The most expensive and famous was Hilda. Introduced in 1914, she was created under several different mould numbers with real or painted hair. This mulatto bisque example is much rarer than the more common white bisque and is worth almost twice as much.
£5,000–6,000

KESTNER & CO

Johannes Daniel Kestner was the founder of the doll industry in Waltershaüsen in Germany in the early 19th century. Under his grandson Adolph, the firm produced bisque-headed child dolls on jointed composition bodies in the 1880s, but did not make character dolls until 1910. Kestner was one of the few German companies that manufactured heads and bodies themselves. Kestner dolls were popular in the United States where they were distributed by George Borgfeldt.

▶ ORIENTAL BABIES

Oriental baby boys are rarer than girls. They have widely spaced, crescent- or almond-shaped eyes and open mouths with teeth. Like all Kestner babies, they are extremely chubby with noticeably fat tummies. They may have a solid domed head with moulded hair, as in this example.
£3,000–4,000

ETHNIC DOLLS

SIMON & HALBIG WERE PROBABLY THE MOST PROLIFIC GERMAN MAKERS OF MULATTO OR BROWN DOLLS, AND SPECIALISTS IN ORIENTAL GIRL DOLLS, WHOSE VALUE MAY BE INCREASED CONSIDERABLY BY AN ORIGINAL EXOTIC COSTUME. DOLLS WITH NEGROID FEATURES AND UNUSUAL MOULD NUMBERS, SUCH AS THE 1902

EXAMPLE PICTURED, ARE AMONG THE MOST VALUABLE OF ALL BISQUE DOLLS. THIS ONE, 16 IN (41 CM) TALL WITH A BALL-JOINTED WOOD AND COMPOSITION BODY, IS IMPRESSED WITH THE MOULD NUMBER 130 ON THE HEAD. THE BROWN GLASS EYES ARE WEIGHTED BY MEANS OF A WIRE ATTACHED TO A PIECE OF LEAD INSIDE THE HEAD.
£20,000–25,000

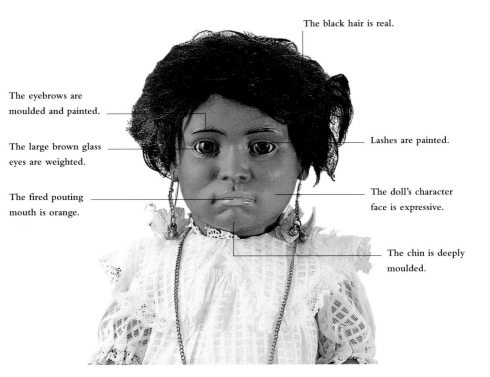

The black hair is real.

The eyebrows are moulded and painted.

The large brown glass eyes are weighted.

Lashes are painted.

The fired pouting mouth is orange.

The doll's character face is expressive.

The chin is deeply moulded.

GERMAN CHARACTER DOLLS II: KÄMMER & REINHARDT

The firm was founded in Waltershausen, Germany, in 1886 by designer and model-maker Ernst Kämmer and entrepreneur Franz Reinhardt. Despite Kämmer's death in 1901, the company was successful and in 1909 it was the first firm to produce a character doll. Pre-First World War character dolls are most wanted, but the firm continued until 1940.

▶ **KAISER BABIES**
This doll is known as a Kaiser baby because it was supposedly modelled on the German Emperor's son. The boy had polio as a child and was left with a crippled hand. The doll is entirely different from earlier idealized babies, with one arm bent inwards and the hand held up giving a rather odd appearance which was unpopular at the time. Legs and toes are carefully modelled with an accentuated big toe. The earliest Kaisers have multi-jointed bodies, but most are the five-piece, bent-limb type. The mould No. 100 was used and all subsequent character dolls are numbered above 100. Brown-eyed Kaisers are rarer, as are babies with a dark skin. £600-700

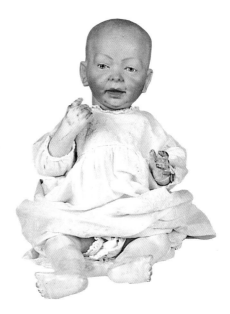

◀ **CHILD CHARACTERS**
Child character dolls are highly collectable and many were recorded with names. Certain moulds were interchangeable as girls or boys, depending on dress and painting of the face. This 1910, 22 in (56 cm) boy known as Carl has typical painted eyes and closed mouth. He is impressed with mould No. 107. £30,000–40,000

BEWARE
Do not confuse dolls of mould Nos. 117 and 117/A (right) with the 117N No. doll which is worth much less. The 117N was made from 1919 and has a much rounder face, an open mouth, upper teeth and flirting eyes. Although popular, its value (depending on size) is only £800–1,200.

▶ **RARE NUMBERS**
The rarest mould numbers such as 107 are very valuable. Some, such as a 106 model of which only 50 are thought to have been made, can be worth £100,000. Other rarities are 102, 103, 104, 105 – and registered but never seen moulds still turn up. The 1909 doll pictured, nearly 22 in (56 cm) tall, with serene expression, painted eyes, open/closed mouth and six-ball-jointed wood and composition body, is the only known No. 108 and was the world price record holder when sold at Sotheby's in 1994. Other mould nos. not seen but registered by the Kämmer & Reinhardt factory are 110, 111 and 113. The high value which is attributed much reflects the doll's uniqueness and if another turned up it is very doubtful that the price would be the same.
£190,000–200,000

◀ **MEIN LIEBLING OR 'MY DARLING'**
Mould Nos. 117 and 117/A, dating from 1911, were a general favourite and they still are among collectors. The dolls have a particularly endearing expression, with a closed, slightly smiling mouth, glass eyes and six-ball-jointed wood and composition body. This example is large, being nearly 32 in (81 cm) tall, but smaller versions were made. The mohair wig was commonly used by the Kämmer & Reinhardt factory rather than real human hair.
£5,000–6,000

MARKS
Look for the manufacturer's stamp on the back of the neck or head under the hairline. Character dolls should also have a number.

GERMAN CHARACTER DOLLS III: ARMAND MARSEILLE

Armand Marseille was a Russian-born doll-maker who first ran a German porcelain factory in Thuringia and then bought a toy factory where, with his son Armand Junior, he was making bisque heads by 1890. They also supplied other companies from 1900 to 1930. Although they were the most prolific of German manufacturers, they are not noted for quality and so are less expensive than other German character dolls.

▼ DREAM BABIES

The Dream Baby, first produced in 1924, was the most popular Armand Marseille baby doll. They were made in vast quantities from life-size to very small, but quality varies. Those with open mouths are marked "351", those with closed mouths are "341". Some have a soft, stuffed body with a squeaker, soft, thickly stuffed legs and composition hands, like the larger doll pictured. Others, like the smaller doll, have a five-piece, bent-limb composition body. A closed mouth, bent-limb composition body and small size is usually preferable. However, in this case the 22 in- (56 cm-) tall doll is pretty enough to be the more valuable.

Large £200–250
Small £150–200

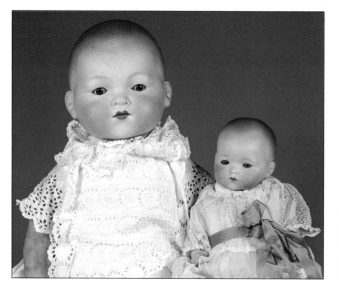

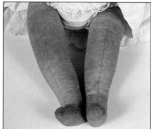

BEWARE

Some soft-bodied Dream Babies have celluloid hands. If damaged, they are impossible to restore – do not be persuaded otherwise. The value is reduced if the body has been replaced. Avoid ruddy, orange bisque.

▶ BLACK BABIES

Black babies were made from the Dream Baby mould. Colouring varies from black painted to coffee-coloured fired bisque. Fired bisque is more desirable and has an eggshell shine. If in doubt, scratch the surface somewhere hidden and paint will come away, leaving a white mark. This is a '341' baby with a fired head. £300–400

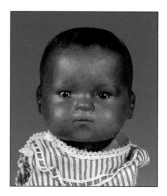

The blonde mohair wig
is attractively styled.

The delicately moulded
face is pale bisque.

MYSTERY BOY

THIS EARLY 20TH-CENTURY
CHARACTER DOLL OF A YOUNG
BOY, ACCOMPANIED BY A STEIFF
DOG, IS AN EXCEPTIONALLY
RARE MODEL BUT SOMETHING
OF A MYSTERY. THE 19 IN
(48 CM) DOLL IS IMPRESSED
WITH THE NUMBER 111 BUT
WITH NO INDICATION OF THE
FACTORY. HOWEVER, IN
ADDITION TO THE FAMOUS
DREAM BABIES AND A VAST
ASSORTMENT OF OTHER
RELATIVELY INEXPENSIVE GIRL
AND CHARACTER DOLLS,
ARMAND MARSEILLE CREATED
A FEW HIGHLY REFINED DOLLS.
THE CHARACTERISTICS OF THIS
DOLL SUGGEST THAT IT COULD
BE ONE OF THEM. SO IN SPITE
OF THREE MISSING FINGERS
AND MINOR WIG DAMAGE, THE
DOLL IS HIGHLY VALUED.
£20,000–25,000

Painted blue eyes
such as these are
unusual.

The closed, slightly
pouting mouth is
another unusual
feature.

Unlike the harsh
colouring used on other
characters, this boy has
subtly blushing cheeks.

The ball-jointed
wood and composi-
tion body is dressed
in the elegant
original outfit.

◀ ORIENTAL BABIES
Armand Marseille made only
one type of yellow-tinted baby
doll and the modelling is much
less lifelike than on Oriental
babies by other firms such as
Kestner. Although this 1925
example is not as attractive
as some dolls, it is still very
collectable and popular.
Some bodies are cloth but this
is composition. £500–600

WHAT TO LOOK FOR

● Armand Marseille
marks, such as a mould
number or the name of
the style – for identification rather than dating.
● Elaborate original
clothes can make a basic
doll seem more valuable.
● Original paint on face
and hands as repainting
reduces the value.

GERMAN CHARACTER DOLLS IV: OTHER MAKERS

The oldest known dollmaking business was Dressel, founded in 1700, which became Cuno & Otto Dressel in 1873 until its closure in 1945. The company had several factories in the Sonneberg area and began making bisque heads in the 1870s but also bought heads from other firms. Franz Schmidt was an innovatory dollmaker from 1890 to 1930 at Georgenthal near Waltershaüsen. The first to make babies with sleeping eyes operated by elastic, he also introduced pierced nostrils in 1912 and trembling tongues in 1914.

▶ **GEBRÜDER HEUBACH**

This firm was founded by the Heubach brothers in 1820 in Thuringia, originally to make porcelain. By 1905, the firm was manufacturing whole dolls. Distinctive, usually pink, bisque heads with exaggerated expressions are their strong point.

In comparison, the bodies are very crudely modelled. Look for highly realistic intaglio eyes, moulded with an indented pupil and iris and then painted, often with a white dot added to the iris for the illusion of extra depth. The 1914 winking doll pictured, although only 9 in (23 cm) tall, is worth £700–800.

▲ **PIANO BABIES**

Gebrüder Heubach was also known for all-bisque figurines of babies intended for display on a piano, hence the name Piano Babies. These and larger mantelpiece babies should bear the Heubach mark. Other firms made similar babies but these are unmarked and much less valuable.
£300–400

▶ **ERNST HEUBACH**

Based in Koppelsdorf, Heubach made inexpensive girl dolls, babies and characters from 1887 to 1930. His daughter Beatrix married Armand Marseille's son. Too-highly coloured cheeks are an immediate clue to a Heubach doll. His black dolls had grass skirts, coloured bead necklaces and bracelets and gold hoop earrings. The smaller doll pictured is in its original skirt. The pair are different sizes, 7 in (18 cm) and 16 in (41 cm) tall, from the same 399 mould, but whereas the larger doll is painted, the smaller is made of brown bisque with the colour fixed by firing and is the more valuable.
Smaller £400
Larger £150

◀ ALT, BECK & GOTTSCHALCK

The Nauendorf-based firm made all-bisque dolls and bisque heads, including 1920s heads for the Bye-lo babies (see pages 136–7). Alt, Beck & Gottschalck dolls have square faces, small features and flat, painted eyebrows. The back view of this head shows the firm's initials and mould number. Foreshortened thighs give a long-legged look known as 'flapper' legs. £300–400

◀ CARL BERGNER

Carl Bergner began making dolls in 1890 in Sonneberg and quickly began to concentrate on multi-face dolls, dated the same year, like the one pictured. The bisque head on a papier-mâché shoulder-plate is attached to composition lower limbs as shown. By a system of pulling strings in the side of the body, the crying face can be changed to a smiling face. £700–800

BEWARE

Most Gebrüder Heubach dolls bear the firm's rising sun mark or "Heubach" incorporated into a square (left). Do not confuse with the horseshoe mark (right) used by the unconnected Ernst Heubach doll company. New dolls are being made out of some old Gebrüder Heubach moulds. These are slightly smaller than the originals as the moulds from which they are produced are taken from original dolls. Prices decreased between 1991–6 by nearly a third, partly because of fear of fakes.

GOOGLY, KEWPIE & BYE-LO DOLLS

Googlies are caricature figures with round, or googly, eyes and impish expressions, stemming from the drawings of Grace Gebbie Drayton, an American illustrator and artist who created the Campbell Kids.

The first googly-eyed dolls with bisque heads were marketed in 1911 and they were continued for over 20 years, made by various major German factories.

Supposedly the guardian angels of children, Kewpies were the inspiration of American illustrator Rose O'Neill, who used line drawings of Cupid-like figures to illustrate stories in the *Ladies' Home Journal* in 1909. Designed under her supervision by Joseph Kallus, the first bisque Kewpies were made by Kestner in 1913. Kewpies were also produced in many other materials, but bisque are the most sought after today. Most have pedestal legs, jointed arms and webbed, starfish hands, just visible 'wings' below the ears and the Rose O'Neill signature on the foot.

GOOGLIES IN COSTUME

THIS UNUSUAL PAIR OF GOOGLIES MADE IN 1914 BY KÄMMER & REINHARDT ARE OF THE FIRM'S TYPICAL HIGH QUALITY WITH ALL THE GOOGLY CHARACTERISTICS.
£2,500–3,000 EACH

The round or 'googly' eyes are sideways glancing.

The snub nose is tiny compared with the huge eyes.

The watermelon-type mouth is closed and only the bottom lip painted.

Short, slanting eyebrows are high on the brow.

◀ **KESTNER**
This Googly made by Kestner is less than 12 in (30 cm) tall and has typical features.
£3,000–4,000

The shoes are a fine example of the attention to detail that makes Googlies so collectable.

Googlies came in a wide assortment of costumes. The more detail visible, the higher the value.

▲ ARMAND MARSEILLE

A less expensive Armand Marseille Googly, mould No. 323, this doll was produced in 1920. She does not have the distinctive Googly smile and is generally less refined. Both wig and clothes are replacements and the chubby toddler body has fixed wrists with starfish hands similar to Kewpie dolls. £500–600

▶ LABELS

This 1920s Kewpie has the circular label pictured attached to its back. Sometimes the label is on the doll's front. It may be heart-shaped or there may be no label at all, just the signature on the foot. Watch out for unauthorized Japanese Kewpies with spurious labels, which may simply bear the labels 'Nippon' or 'Foreign'. This unidentified Kewpie is worth £100–200

▼ RARE KESTNERS

This is a particularly rare 1913 Kewpie with glass eyes instead of the usual painted variety, a five-piece composition body and the marks of Kestner as well as the O'Neill signature. £3,000–3,500

BYE-LOS

Bye-los were designed by an American art teacher, Grace Storey Putnam, in 1922 and nicknamed 'the million-dollar babies' because of the overwhelming demand for them. They were modelled on a newborn child with half-closed eyes and creased limbs – and made in different materials from original life-size to miniature examples, with varying features. All-bisque Bye-los are marked "Copr Grace S. Putnam, Germany" on the body, and are numbered according to size. This typical Kestner miniature has painted eyes and hair, jointed limbs and a realistically splayed body. £600–800

FABRIC & RAG DOLLS I

Fabric dolls have been made since the earliest times. Safe, soft for cuddling and as cheap as required, they were sometimes little more than a treasured bundle of rags. Being fabric, few have survived the rigors of playtime or ravaging of moths. As they were cheap, they were usually thrown away and replaced. The first significant survivors date from the second half of the 19th century.

English wax dollmakers Madame Montanari, Pierotti and John Edwards all made cloth dolls, and by the beginning of the 20th century several leading manufacturers were producing dolls based on famous personalities, fictional and real. Norah Wellings was the most prolific. In the United States, the big 19th-century names were Izannah Walker and Martha Chase, followed by J.B. Sheppard & Co of Philadelphia with their Philadelphia Babies. Top German producers were teddy-bear inventor Margarete Steiff and Käthe Kruse whose dolls were modelled like Bye-los on newborn babies. In Italy, Lenci made very elegant dolls for adults.

Today the price of cloth dolls varies widely. The most expensive are Martha Chase, Izannah Walker, Käthe Kruse and Steiff, plus 1920s and 1930s Lenci. Norah Wellings and other English makers are the cheapest. With regard to the value of fabric dolls, much depends on condition as restoration is difficult and many cannot even be washed.

FLORENCE UPTON

Florence Upton, born to English parents in New York in 1873, illustrated *The Adventures of Two Dutch Dolls and a Golliwogg* (1895) with a black rag-doll character. Verses were by her mother, Bertha. Golliwogg had a big smile, fuzzy hair and staring, white-rimmed eyes. He wore a stand-up collar, bow-tie and brightly coloured jacket and trousers. The doll upon which Florence based her drawings was sold for charity in the First World War and is now at the British Prime Minister's residence, Chequers.

ROBERTSON'S BROOCHES

Gollies were so popular that Robertson's, jam and preserve manufacturers adopted the figure as their symbol in 1910 and in 1928 introduced enamel Golly brooches which could be sent for in return for buying their products. Halted in 1939 as the metal was required for the war effort, the scheme was relaunched in 1945. The Robertson's golly also appeared in felt cut-out form and 1950s examples can be worth £15– 25.

▼ **GOLLY REVIVAL**
Gollies, which went out of fashion due to their political incorrectness, are enjoying a comeback following the 100th anniversary of their creation in 1895. Many companies produced them and the best to look out for are by Steiff which can be worth £3,000–4,000.

▶ **MARKS AND LABELS**
Käthe Kruse dolls were always marked on the left foot with a signature and number, although this may no longer be decipherable. The first dolls had labels on their wrists. From 1928 these were placed round the neck. Modern dolls also have the name and number on one foot, but the tell-tale clue is the label with the shield trademark around the neck. £1,000–1,500

◀ **BODY CHARACTERISTICS**
Bodies were made from cloth which had been treated with chemicals so that it would be washable. The earlier dolls had a navel, wide hips and five seams to the leg to create a realistic shape. Narrow-hipped bodies came in from 1930.
£1,500–2,000

WHAT TO LOOK FOR
• Early dolls' heads were moulded from calico with three hand-stitched pate seams. Hair and features were painted with oils
• After 1929 dolls have one pate seam.
• From 1935 some heads were made of magnesite (a plaster substitute).
• Hollow swivel heads of covered cardboard were introduced after the Second World War.
• Celluloid and plastic took over in 1950.

KÄTHE KRUSE
Käthe Kruse set out to design dolls that were safe, unbreakable, washable and attractive to children. The first were made in 1909 by Kämmer & Reinhardt, but, unhappy with their quality, she was producing them in her own workshop at Bad Kosen by 1912 and after 1945 in her Donauwörth factory. She died in 1968 but her dolls are still made. This 1920 doll, almost 17 in (43 cm) tall, was the only type made until 1922 after which it was produced alongside other models. £800–1,000

FABRIC & RAG DOLLS II: STEIFF

Teddy-bear inventor Margarete Steiff first began making felt toys with remnants from a factory near her home in Giengen, Wurtenburg, south Germany (see also p.48).

Margarete set up in business with her nephew Richard Steiff and by 1903 had toy outlets in Berlin, Hamburg, Leipzig, London, Paris, Amsterdam and Florence. In 1908 she was employing 2,000 workers, but still claimed to examine every doll they made. The company has continued since her death in 1909.

▲ DACHAU PEASANTS
Steiff had a great penchant for comic figures. These 1911 musicians known as Dachau Peasants are especially rare. Their black-button eyes and large feet are typical of Steiff character dolls. But their integral ears and horizontal facial seams are unusual, as is the presence of Steiff buttons in both ears and on their costume. £1,500–2,000 each

WHAT TO LOOK FOR
• Bodies were made all or partially from felt stuffed with wood-shavings until 1908.
• From 1909 plush and velvet were sometimes used instead of felt.
• Heads and hands were always covered in felt, even if the bodies were not.

MARKS

Because Margarete Steiff's first success was with a felt elephant-shaped pin-cushion, she chose the animal, its trunk curling to form a letter 'S', as her trademark. At first she used paper labels, then in 1904 introduced metal ear buttons either blank or embossed with an elephant as shown. From 1905, the button was printed with "Steiff" and in 1908 they had a cloth label underneath bearing a product number. Blue-plated or blank tin buttons were sometimes used during the Second World War. If the identifying buttons have been removed, the residual holes should still be visible.

REGIONAL DRESS

THIS 1913 DOLL, 13IN (33CM) TALL, INCLUDES MANY TYPICAL STEIFF FEATURES.
£600–800

Facial details are painted.

Button eyes are typical.

The ears are not integral but applied.

The seaming runs vertically down the centre of the face.

Large feet enable the doll to stand.

◀ MASS ATTRACTION

Steiff were one of many makers to start producing gollies. This character was made by Steiff in 1913. He is marked with the button in his left ear and the original felt clothes are in good condition. He is 17 in (43cm) tall with excelsior stuffing. He has black, shoe-button eyes backed by black-and-white felt discs. £5,000–6,000

REPRODUCTIONS & FORGERIES

Limited editions of earlier dolls use the button adopted since 1986 with "Steiff" in cursive script. Forged buttons are generally reserved for Steiff teddy bears, as these are more valuable than Steiff dolls.

FABRIC & RAG DOLLS III: NORAH WELLINGS

Initially a designer for Chad Valley, Norah Wellings established her own soft-toy factory in Wellington, Shropshire, in 1926. Her brother Leonard managed the business side while she concentrated on the design and production. Wellings patented a form of doll's head made of fabric or felt backed with buckram (stiffened cloth) and incorporating also some 'plastic' wood.

The dolls she created were chiefly character dolls and she looked upon them as her family, which is probably why her designs were more successful than those of some larger manufacturers. Output continued until 1960.

▶ **CHARACTERISTICS**
Costumes are always strongly coloured. Heads are well modelled, especially on the large dolls such as this 1935 example which is almost 30 in (76 cm) tall. The face is pressed brown velvet, although others may be slightly rough felt, in which case the body may be cloth. Eyes were sometimes painted; these are glass and are, typically, glancing sideways. The eyebrows are lightly painted in a single line and the ears are applied. Dolls' heads were given a waterproof coating so that their faces were washable. £300–350

MARKS
All Miss Wellings' dolls were set out with a cloth label either on a wrist or under a foot saying "Made in England by Norah Wellings".

WHAT TO LOOK FOR
● So many dolls were made by Norah Wellings that they are easily available and, although their quality is high, many are inexpensive.
● For this reason, condition and original clothing are extremely important.

► **CHARACTERS**
These two North American
Indian brown velvet dolls, each
12 in (30 cm) tall and in brightly
coloured felt costumes, are
typical of the wide range of
character dolls Norah Wellings
produced. Others include
Britannia with a quilted, plumed
fabric helmet and coat of mail,
Little Bo Peep, South-Sea
Islanders, Canadian Mounties,
Sailors and Cowboys. The Jolly
Toddlers began in 1933. These
are a good collectable at only
£100–150 each.

◄ **MASCOTS**
Many of Norah Wellings' dolls
were sold as mascots on board
American ocean liners. She
made a Harry the Hawk doll for
sale in aid of Royal Airforce
comforts during the Second
World War, and a model called
Cora, designed for presentation
to Queen Mary who visited the
factory in 1927. The Noreen
range of foreign dolls, such as
the 33 in- (84 cm-) tall Dutch
boy pictured, was introduced in
1937. This doll, which has a
distinct Lenci influence, is more
expensive. £300–400
(The top-priced dolls are those
modelled on the Royal Family
or other famous people. These
can fetch £500–800.)

**WHAT TO
LOOK FOR**

- Cloth label sewn to
the wrist or foot.
- Applied ears.
- Sculpted faces.
- Zig-zag stitching on
the head.
- Attention to detail
denotes better dolls.
- Colourful, original
clothing.

FABRIC & RAG DOLLS IV: OTHER BRITISH MAKERS

British manufacturers' fabric and rag dolls generally fall into the lower price categories. Many dolls were inspired by characters in children's literature such as Mabel Lucie Attwell's babies. The Royal Family was also frequently portrayed by dollmakers, the young princesses being especially popular. Many dolls had the reassuring words "Hygienic Toy" incorporated in their labels, as rivalry among toymakers grew. As a result of the fact that these doll were mass-produced, however, they are relatively easy to find.

CHAD VALLEY MARKS

Most 1920s and 1930s dolls are marked "Hygienic Toys Made in England by Chad Valley Toy Company Ltd". After 1938, some dolls were labelled "Toy Makers to H.M. The Queen," which changed to "...the Queen Mother" after the coronation in 1953.

◀ PRINCESS ELIZABETH

Chad Valley was particularly famous for portraying the English princesses Elizabeth and Margaret. In 1930 a model of Elizabeth was sold for one guinea at the express wish of her parents, the Duke and Duchess of York, who thought the doll should not be too expensive for people of average means. This 1938 version has a typically fine moulded felt face with glass eyes, mohair wig and stuffed velvet body. The clothes are copies of the originals. £100; in original clothes £400–600.

◀ CHAD VALLEY CO LTD

Founded in Birmingham in 1823 and still in existence, the firm began as a printing and bookbinding business. The name stems from the Chad stream which ran beside one of the firm's factories. The firm began producing soft toys and dolls in about 1920, specializing in already popularized characters such as Mabel Lucie Attwell dolls, Snow White and portrait dolls of royal children. They developed a reputation for high-quality materials and workmanship, using plush, velvet, felt, stockinette and other fabrics – and they claimed their dolls were hygienically stuffed. This 1923 doll is in particularly good condition. £100–150

BEWARE

Cloth dolls are susceptible to damage from moths as well as from being cuddly playthings. As they are difficult to restore satisfactorily, condition is important to their value.

J.K. FARNELL & CO

A LONDON FIRM (1871–1968), J.K. FARNELL
& CO INITIALLY PRODUCED SOFT TOYS AT THE
ALPHA WORKS, ACTON HILL. BY 1925, ARTIST
CHLOE PRESTON WAS DESIGNING DOLLS FOR
FARNELL IN MODERN MATERIALS. THE COMPANY
PRODUCED VARIOUS ALPHA RANGES OF DOLL
IN THE 1930s OF WHICH THIS ONE IS TYPICAL.
ALTHOUGH DRESSED ONLY IN PYJAMAS AND
DRESSING GOWN, SHE WOULD ORIGINALLY HAVE
HAD A DAY DRESS, SHOES, HAT AND COAT TO
COMPLETE HER WARDROBE. £200–300

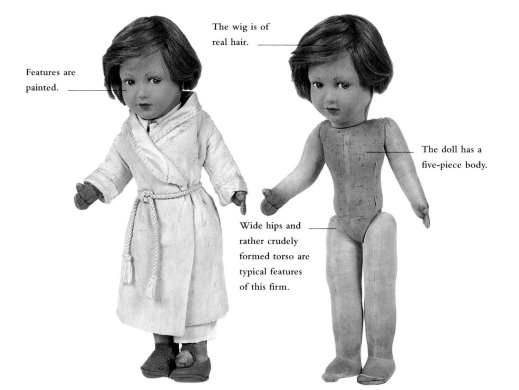

Features are
painted.

The wig is of
real hair.

The doll has a
five-piece body.

Wide hips and
rather crudely
formed torso are
typical features
of this firm.

▶ **DEAN'S RAG BOOK
CO LTD**
Founded in London in 1905 to
print rag books and dolls, the
first dolls were printed on
material to be made up at
home. Moulded felt dolls were
made from 1920 onwards
including Princess, Smart Set,
Frilly and Sunshine dolls.
Children's illustrators such as
Hilda Cowham were employed
to design several of the dolls. A
few have been reproduced
recently, among them a 1923
Dismal Desmond and a 1920
Charlie Chaplin. Printed shoes
and socks are a characteristic
feature. Many Dean's dolls bear
the oval stamp of a terrier
fighting a bulldog for a rag
book, sometimes inscribed
"Hygienic A1 toys, made in
England, Dean's Rag Book Co.
Ltd". This doll is from the
Evripose line introduced in
1923 and was probably made a
few years later. £100–150

FABRIC & RAG DOLLS V: LENCI

An Italian company based in Turin, Lenci was founded in 1908 by Enrico di Scavini. Scavini named the company after his pet name for his wife Elan Konig. The dolls he produced were the first so-called art dolls and would appeal to anyone over age five. Many were designed by leading Italian artists and each was looked upon as an individual work of art. Made of moulded felt with jointed bodies, the dolls had very expressive faces, often with painted eyes. Since the dolls were intended for display, their costume is all-important. The most sought after were made 1920–1941, although Lenci dolls are still made today.

◀ BOY DOLLS
This 1930 Italian Officer doll is jointed at shoulders and hips and has a swivelling neck. Note the lighter pink spot on the lower lip. £1,500–1,750

▲ NATIONAL COSTUME
National costume was an opportunity for Lenci to produce elaborate and colourful design, as in the case of this 41 in- (104 cm-) tall and particularly fine Russian lady made in the 1930s.

Characteristic features which help to identify her are the two white dots painted in her eyes (although this was sometimes imitated by Norah Wellings) and the colour of the lower lip, which is paler than the upper lip. £2,000–2,500

▶ HAND CLUES
Separately stitched outer fingers and two inner fingers joined together is an indication of a Lenci doll.

BEWARE
Now that Lenci dolls are becoming more expensive, increasing instances are coming to light of spurious pewter buttons attached to recent dolls by unscrupulous dealers to suggest that the dolls are valuable examples from the 1920s.

▶ **ORGANDIE**
A translucent form of muslin, organdie, was used particularly effectively in Lenci costumes. The delicate, diaphanous nature of the material was ideal for producing extravagant puff sleeves, flowering trains and creating masses of layered frills. Note also the expressive sideways glance of this 1930 doll, who is wearing an original organdie blouse of the time.
£500–600

◀ **PATCHWORK**
Patchwork was favoured with Lenci designers because it gave them the chance to experiment with colour effects. This 1930 doll is a typical Lenci and has frilly sleeves and matching muslin pantaloons. The round, surprised eyes are glass rather than painted and therefore more valuable.
£2,500–3,000

▶ **ZIGZAG CLUE**
A zigzagged seam at the back of the head is distinctively 'Lenci'. Jointing of the hips is more sophisticated than the copies which cheaply "bolt" the leg to the torso, by a nail.

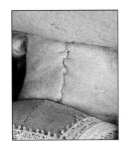

WHAT TO LOOK FOR
• All but a few early dolls are marked. 1920s and 1930s dolls were stamped in black or purple on the foot and 1930s dolls also had model numbers, which began at 100, on their labels.
• Dolls with the same model number wore the same clothes in different colours.
• Cardboard tags instead of paper labels were introduced in 1938. Some early dolls have a pewter button marked "Lenci" attached to their clothes.
• From 1925–50, ribbons with the company name were sewn into Lenci garments.

FABRIC & RAG DOLLS VI: NORTH AMERICAN MAKERS

The tradition of cloth dolls is strong in North America. The playthings of early European settlers' children in the 17th century, homemade versions were created out of scraps of material. Early dolls thus have an additional collectability as folk art. Commercial production began with such makers as Izannah Walker in the second half of the 19th century but did not take off in an important way until the beginning of the 20th century.

▶ IZANNAH F. WALKER

Based at Central Falls, Rhode Island, from the middle of the 19th century, Izannah F. Walker was a female dollmaker whose dolls are highly collectable today. All the dolls have oil-painted features, including this example, one of the first produced and extremely rare today. Typically, the doll has a closed mouth, painted brown eyes and hair, applied ears and a cloth body. The doll is wearing an original brown and red striped dress, a wired green silk and gauze bonnet and red leather shoes. £4,000–5,000

Unusually, this doll has painted, ringleted hair. Most have painted curls round the ears.

Hands stitched with separate thumbs are characteristic of Izannah Walker dolls.

MARTHA JENKS CHASE

Martha Jenks Chase of Pawtucket, Rhode Island made some mask-faced stockinette dolls with white sateen or cotton bodies for her children. The dolls' success led to the establishment in the 1880s of the Chase Stockinette Doll Company which was continued by the family until 1925. Typical dolls have oil-painted features, applied ears, brightly painted eyes, thick upper lashes and painted hair. Early bodies have seams at knee, hip, elbow and shoulder – while the later ones have joints only at the shoulder and hip. Some bear a paper label; others are stamped on the left leg or arm.

PAWTUCKET, R.I
MADE IN U.S.A.

The use of patterned cotton to cover the body is another very typical feature.

▶ **DEEP SOUTH**

These two black lady dolls are typical of dolls which are made in the southern states of North America and they are highly collectable today. Their maker is unknown, but they probably date from c.1880 and are very well made. The faces and bodies are stitched and they are wearing colourful clothes. The formed bosoms have stitched red nipples. £600–800 each

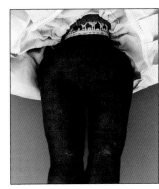

The detail on these dolls adds greatly to their value. Note the rings on the fingers, made from sewn-on beads. Sequins and beads are also applied to the forearms and around the neck. The fingernails are made of split porcupine quills and stitching of the fingers is all individually finished. The dolls usually have large hips and wear small, heeled, silk slippers.

▶ **RAGGEDY DOLLS**

John Gruelle wrote a story based on a rag doll found by his daughter in an attic, and the family produced about 200 Raggedy Ann dolls with a wooden heart and six lower lashes on hand-painted faces. In 1918, Volland & Co began to produce the dolls. Raggedy Andy was created in 1920. Second versions appeared in the 1920s with printed face and four eyelashes. This pair are typical of those made between 1938 and 1968 by the Georgene Novelty Co, part of Averill Manufacturing. £80–100

CELLULOID DOLLS

The trade name for cellulose and powdered camphor, celluloid, was patented in North America in 1869, originally for manufacturing billiard balls. The Rheinische Gummiund Celluloid Fabrik Co of Bavaria used celluloid as early as 1873 as a cheap alternative to bisque. Other manufacturers followed suit, often using the same mould for both materials. However, although not susceptible to flaking and peeling, celluloid is flammable, easily cracked or dented and likely to fade. Consequently, the condition of celluloid dolls is particularly important to its value. Leading makes in Germany and France were Kestner, Kämmer & Reinhardt and Jumeau. Celluloid dolls were made in smaller numbers in England, and also in the United States by E.I. Horsman and Averill. Dolls were modelled as both babies and children, and they are most characterized by a glossy sheen on the face.

◀ **CONDITION**
Condition is vitally important since celluloid is almost impossible to restore. This 1950 moulded German doll was probably sold as a souvenir of Bavaria. Curiously, although it is in excellent condition, it is not very valuable as it is a less popular design. £30–50

▶ **RHEINISCHE GUMMIUND CELLULOID FABRIK CO**
This all-celluloid doll has a jointed toddler body and was made around 1930. The dress is not original. £200–300

▶ **COLLECTORS' FAVOURITES**
Celluloid dolls are accessible to most collectors since so many were produced and they were in the lower price range from the start. Kestner character dolls are especially sought after, plus dolls with glass eyes or with original clothes, preferably made 1910–1915. This example is a good-quality, all-celluloid 1930 French doll, with a swivel head, moulded and painted hair and original glass eyes. £300–400

► MARKS

Most celluloid dolls are marked, sometimes twice if a celluloid firm used another dollmaker's mould. The most famous mark is a turtle which the Rheinische Gummiund Celluloid Fabrik Company adopted in 1889 as a symbol of the durability and longevity of their dolls. After 1899, the turtle was enclosed in a lozenge shape with the word "Schutzmarke", meaning trademark, beneath. Other common marks include "S.I.C" (*Société Industrielle de Celluloid*) and an eagle surmounting the word "France". Sometimes there are the initials "S.N.F." in a diamond.

THIS IS A 1920 GERMAN DOLL BY KAMMER & REINHARDT AND IS MODELLED AS A CHILD. MODELS OF BOTH BABIES AND CHILDREN WERE PRODUCED AND THE DOLLS HAVE EITHER A SWIVEL HEAD ON A CELLULOID OR COMPOSITION BODY OR, LIKE THIS ONE, A SHOULDER-HEAD ATTACHED TO A SOFT BODY WITH CELLULOID LOWER LIMBS.

THE HAIR MAY BE MOULDED AND PAINTED OR A WIG (DOLLS WITH WIGS WERE MORE EXPENSIVE ORIGINALLY), BUT ONLY THE BETTER QUALITY DOLLS HAVE GLASS EYES. THE CELLULOID TENDS TO HAVE A GLOSSY SHEEN AND THESE DOLLS ARE LIGHTER IN WEIGHT THAN HARD PLASTIC. RUBBED AGAINST CLOTHING, THE CELLULOID MAY SMELL OF CAMPHOR. £200–300

Weighted blue glass eyes greatly increase the desirability of this doll.

The wig is made of real hair, which was an important selling point when it was made.

A kid body is typical with a shoulder-head.

Where lower limbs may be visible beneath clothing, they are celluloid.

BEWARE

Celluloid is easily damaged, so check for any cracking, denting or fading as a result of exposure to light. Sadly, a doll which has been too well loved may be of little value to another collector. Poorly defined fingers and toes are characteristic of less valuable dolls.

COMPOSITION DOLLS

Used from the late-19th century until the Second World War in Europe, and especially in America, composition was a less expensive alternative to bisque. It was made from wood or paper pulp which was mixed with rein-forcing ingredients such as rags, bones and eggs. In North America, it was often combined with wood and plastic. North American designers were more adventurous with composition than other countries and

	BETTY BOOP	SKIPPY	ADVERTISING DOLLS
	1935, £80–100	1935, £60–80 each	1935, £300–400 a pair
HOW, WHEN & WHERE	Joseph Kallus, president of The Cameo Doll Co, designed a Betty Boop doll in 1932 based on a well-known cartoon character. The material was wood-pulp composition. Other figures included Baby Bo Kaye and Little Annie Rooney.	EFFanBEE Toy Co, one of America's top manufacturers of 'unbreakable' composition dolls focused on Skippy, a comic-strip figure created by Percy L. Crosby and played in a subsequent film by Jackie Cooper. These were called 'Jackie Cooper dolls'.	Many dolls originally created as advertising novelties developed a life of their own. English manufacturers were not as keen on composition as Americans but produced a number of popular and striking dolls such as the Bisto Kids.
WHAT TO LOOK FOR	• An over-sized swivel head with moulded, knobbly hair and painted features. • Large, round eyes. • Jointed body, which might be wooden or composition, moulded as a bathing suit.	• These 1930 dolls have jointed composition bodies along with moulded and painted hair. • Check for chubby cheeks, sideways-glancing, painted eyes, little snub noses and rosebud mouths.	• The more novel and apposite the doll (and his or her facial expression), the better it will be liked – and the higher the value is likely to be. • Curiosity value alone makes them very collectable.

frequently based dolls on popular cartoon figures, advertising characters and current celebrities. These are more sought after than European composition dolls. Owing to the huge variety of composition dolls produced, there are no easy rules for identifying them. The most effective method is familiarity with the type – and there are plenty about. Look carefully at small details. For value, go for the liveliest-looking characters.

HUG-ME-KIDDIES	GERMANIC IDEAL	TOPSY	
1935, £80–100	1930, £20–30	1950, £20–30	
Cheap, googly-eyed Hug-Me-Kiddies were the inspiration of Leon Rees, a Bavarian who became a toymaker in London. These were among his first creations in 1912, crudely made and dressed as both boys and girls, but most appealing due to their naughty expressions.	Idealized rather than exaggerated features were preferred by many German makers in the first half of the 20th century. This 1930 example is typical, and the dolls were manufactured in large quantities.	This black composition doll named Topsy is a character from the *Little Black Sambo* books. Topsies were produced by several companies, including Rosebud English from the 1930s to the 1950s.	HOW, WHEN & WHERE
• Heads are composition. • Eyes move around when operated by a lever. • The body is made of pink felt and the hands are distinctly stubby. • The value increases with the 'naughtiness' of the expression.	• The face should be as traditionally babyish as possible. • Beware of damaged dolls, which are numerous, as these were great favourites with small children.	• The better examples have defined fingers and also extrovert hairstyles. • Avoid dolls whose hair has been lost. • As ever, the doll is more valuable if she has her original clothes.	WHAT TO LOOK FOR

CELEBRITY DOLLS

Movies captured the pre-Second World War imagination so strongly that dollmakers hit upon the idea of portrait dolls of film stars, the more glamorous the better. In post-war days pop stars such as the Beatles have proved pre-eminent. The same celebrities have been portrayed by different manufacturers in several different materials, so there are no easy guidelines. Provided that the quality and condition of the dolls are good, it is the popularity of the celebrity that counts. Look out for them in collections of memorabilia.

▶ **SHIRLEY TEMPLE**
Shirley Temple, the most popular celebrity doll ever made, was first produced in 1934 by the American Ideal Toy & Novelty Co. The dolls were manufactured in 12 sizes. Early dolls mostly had jointed, composition toddler bodies, brown glass sleep eyes and an open mouth with teeth. Some have eyes of enamelled tin – but the best are those with glass flirty eyes. Ideal also produced a small number of Shirley Temple babies and, in 1937, a version in the form of a Polynesian beauty. A vinyl version was made in 1967. This is a 1935 version. £150–200

▲ **DEANNA DURBIN**
Deanna Durbin, film star and singer, was another Ideal favourite. This 1938 doll in composition and wood has a swivel head, real hair (1930s style), sleep eyes and an open mouth with teeth. Sizes range from 14 in (34 cm) to 25 in (64 cm). The doll is less common than Shirley Temple and commands higher prices in North America than in Britain. £200–400

WHAT TO LOOK FOR
● A mark on the head or shoulder-plate and body and possibly a badge bearing a photograph of Shirley Temple.
● The most sought after are the Ideal composition dolls, especially with their original box. Vinyl is less desirable.

▶ **ROYAL CHILDREN**
Typical souvenirs
of the coronation of
Queen Elizabeth II
in 1953, these dolls
representing Prince
Charles and Princess
Anne are by Martha
Thompson, an
American. They are
made of bisque with
cloth bodies, and
stand about 12 in
tall. Produced about
1955, these dolls are
difficult to find and
extremely popular with
American collectors.
Very collectable.
£900–1,000

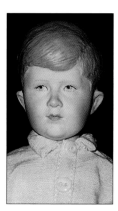

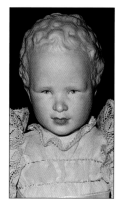

◀ **JOSEPHINE BAKER**
This remarkable
American woman was
renowned as the sexiest
cabaret artiste of the
1920s and later was
famous for her
extensive adopted
family which she
housed in a French
château. Made c.1927,
this Lenci doll (No.
554) is in excellent
condition and would
be highly desired.
£2,500–3,000

▼ **THE BEATLES**
The influence of the
Beatles on fashions in
the 1960s, from
collarless jackets to
elastic-sided Chelsea
boots, and the almost
religious fervour of the
Fab Four's following
made their incarnation
as dolls more or less
inevitable. Many
North American
manufacturers made
vinyl, plastic and
porcelain figurines of
the Beatles. The most
sought after were made
in 1964 by Carmascot,
with composition
heads and real hair.
The heads of the dolls
pictured move on a
spring attached
through the neck.
Known as 'Bobb'n
Beatles', their value
increases if they are
mint and boxed:
without the box their
value would be halved.
£400–500

PLASTIC & VINYL DOLLS I

After the Second World War durable and inexpensive hard plastic was substituted for composition and celluloid, but by the 1950s manufacturers had turned to vinyl which was softer but sometimes liable to fade if left in the sun. Vast quantities were being made so only high-quality dolls are worth collecting. Only rare models in pristine condition are likely to be worth over £100.

Among the best-known makers of early plastic and vinyl was Madame Alexander. Based in North America, Beatrice Behrman, the daughter of Russian-born toymaker

Maurice Alexander, first designed and helped her father to make Red Cross Nurse dolls during the First World War. In 1923 she set up the Alexander Doll Co, trading as Madame Alexander, but she became famous for her hard plastic and vinyl dolls only after 1945. The dolls all had names although different types were from the same moulds. Identified by the name of the first doll produced from each mould, the most common include Margaret, Maggie and Cissie. The most popular type are the Little Women Dolls. Elaborate dresses add greatly to the value.

LABELS

Dolls were generally marked on the head or body with just "Alex", "Alexander" or "Mme Alexander". Some, as in the case of Amy, pictured, have name-tags on their clothes.

▲ LITTLE WOMEN DOLLS

Louisa May Alcott's *Little Women* had no illustrations so Madame Alexander decided to create Meg, Beth, Jo and Amy in doll form. Her Little Women, which were also produced in cloth, are now among the most sought-after hard

plastic dolls and may have the same type of face as either a Margaret or a Maggie doll. The five Little Women dolls pictured are all 14 in tall (36 cm) tall with closed mouth, weighted blue eyes, five-piece body and original costumes and hat boxes.
£700–800 a set

▶ **ROSEBUD**

This black British doll was made by the Northamptonshire dollmaker T. Eric Smith, who registered under the trademark Rosebud. The company is so-named because of a little girl who was presented with a doll after visiting his factory, Nene Plastics. Asked what she most liked about the doll, she replied: "What lovely rosebud lips the doll has". The firm merged with American Mattel Inc in 1967. £40–45

◀ **PEDIGREE**

This is a 1950s all-plastic walking doll with flirty eyes which move from side-to-side if the head is shaken. She was made by Pedigree Soft Toys of London, the firm responsible for Sindy and since taken over first by Dunbee Combex Marx and then Tamwade. She is wearing her original sundress which adds to her value. A particular feature of these dolls was that children could shampoo their hair without damaging the doll. £80–85

MARKS

Note the British National Dolls mark on the back of the head. The back shows the holes of a voice box that emits a sound when the doll is tilted back.

◀▶ **BRITISH NATIONAL DOLLS LTD**

This is a typical good-quality, early 1950s doll by British National Dolls, a London company that specialized in new-born babies. The value of the doll would increase if she still had her original clothes. £40–45

PLASTIC & VINYL DOLLS II: BARBIE

Introduced in 1959 by Mattel, based in Hawthorne, California, Barbie was the first and probably most successful teenage fashion doll ever made. Today, Barbies have acquired a massive following with collectors, with rare early examples fetching thousands of pounds at auction. Most dolls, however, are worth much less. Examples from the early 1960s in good condition and wearing immaculate outfits fetch up to £35 and £40, while later versions and dolls that have been worn by play are worth only a few pounds.

◀ FRIENDS
Various friends were created for Barbie, including Stacey, Skooter and Ken, who is dressed here in an Arabian Nights fancy dress outfit. He was first produced in 1963, although this one dates from the late 1960s. Barbie's friends are traditionally worth less than Barbie, but, since they are rarer, they are becoming increasingly sought after.
£15–20

▶ PACKAGING
An original Mattel box can double the value of any Barbie doll, while mint condition is vital in a recently made example. Although her value would be only a few pounds if her box had been lost and she had been played with, this 1988 mint-and-boxed Black Ballerina is worth between £30 and £35.

COUTURE PERIOD
Barbie's success was due, in part, to the range and quality of her wardrobe. Dolls from 1959–69 (the 'Couture Period') had clothes inspired by haute couture houses such as Balenciaga, Dior and Givenchy. Wardrobes were made especially for Barbie's clothes and some garments are worth more than the basic body. Look for the distinctive Barbie label, as clothes may have been swapped with other makes of doll of the same size. The rarest outfits alone can now cost hundreds of pounds, among them 'Gay Parisienne' and 'American Stewardess', both of which typify the affluence of the post-war American economic boom.

AMERICAN GLAMOUR

THIS 1966 BARBIE
EPITOMIZES THE IMAGE
OF THE POST-WAR
AMERICAN DREAM:
SHE IS GLAMOROUS,
WEALTHY AND
ATTRACTIVE. £35–40

Barbie dolls offered
the chance to buy a
complete lifestyle in
miniature. As well as
numerous outfits,
handbags and shoes,
Barbie had a toy dog
and even a suite of
bedroom furniture.

This elegant evening
dress came complete
with gloves.

If a Barbie has holes in
the feet for a stand, this
indicates she is one of
the first dolls made. This
feature was phased out
by 1961.

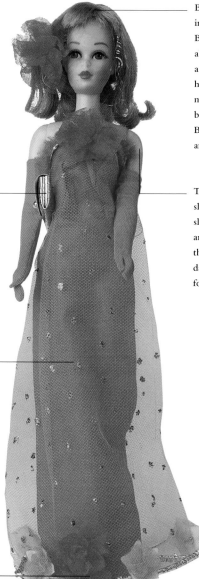

Barbie's fashionable hairstyle was
inspired by Jackie Kennedy.
Barbie's hair is rooted, as with
all vinyl dolls. Early dolls wore
a pony tail, but by 1961 her
hairstyle had developed into a
much more sophisticated bouffant
bubble-cut. Titian and brunette
Barbies are rarer than blondes
and considered more valuable.

The original Barbie dolls had a
slightly oriental look – with
slanting eyes, arched eyebrows
and a pale complexion. During
the 1960s their skin-tone became
darker, reflecting the fashion
for sun tans.

BEWARE
Dolls are sometimes
tampered with. Look
out for recently
drilled holes in the
feet which will not
have acquired the
grime of age. Copies
of Barbies are being
made in the Far East
and these dolls are of
poor quality. Note
that they do not
carry a maker's mark.

WHAT TO LOOK FOR
• The maker's mark is usually
on Barbie's bottom, or
occasionally placed on the back
of a shoulder.
• All real Barbies are marked.

PLASTIC & VINYL DOLLS III: SINDY

The best-selling teenage fashion doll yet made in Britain, Sindy was created by Dennis Arkinstall of Pedigree in 1962. Although intended as a rival to the North American success, Barbie (see pages 158–9), she was originally modelled on an adolescent girl. In 1971 a more sophisticated version was introduced, with a glamorous, long flick-up hair-style instead of the original short version to which a hair piece could be added.

By 1966, Sindy had both a little sister called Patch and a handsome boyfriend named Paul. Both had similarly fashionable outfits designed for them and Paul's often matched Sindy's. Patch was discontinued in the early 1970s and other minor friends have also come and gone.

▼ CLOTHES

Sindy was promoted on television as: "The doll you love to dress" and Pedigree produced a new collection for her every six months. The outfits were made in Hong Kong and embroidered labels sewn into each garment. This early Sindy was made between 1962 and 1966 and is dressed casually in a suede jacket. £10–15

▼ CONDITION

This party-going c.1975 Sindy in a red heart dress would be worth more in mint condition. But, as with many dolls, she has been loved too much and carried everywhere by the hair. Her thinning hair reduces her value. £10–15

▲ BODY

Until 1966, Sindy had plain eyes with straight limbs. Bendable limbs were introduced later and in 1968, when this Sindy was made, realistic eyelashes were added. In 1971 the first 'walking' Sindy was produced with moving head, shoulders, elbows, waist, hips and knees. £20–25

◀ SINDY ACCESSORIES
A huge range of Sindy accessories was produced in the early 1970s including a fully equipped kitchen, bedroom, fillable bath and a grand piano. For out-of-doors she had a chestnut horse called Peanuts and a battery-operated scooter. Many of these items are highly collectable. £15–20

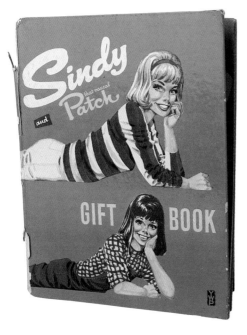

◀ SINDY BOOKS
As Sindy's popularity escalated, a Christmas annual was brought out. This book dates from 1966. It must be in good condition to be worth £25–30.

▼ BLACK SINDY
Only 250 black Sindys were ever made. This 1977 model in her original box is among the most valuable Sindys available. £20–25

MARKS
Look for the identification mark under the hair on the back of the head on all Sindy dolls.

PLASTIC & VINYL DOLLS IV:
ACTION MAN & LATER DOLLS

The most distinctive recent dolls are the ones to collect. Best of all are those which have not been taken out of their boxes. If boxes are lost or the the dolls are in any way damaged, their value will immediately plummet. Few are worth over £100 and most only around £20.

▲ ACTION MAN

The Action Man doll stemmed from GI Joe, a doll produced by Hasbro in America and the first doll specifically designed for boys. As with Barbie and Sindy, the appeal arose from his variety of outfits. These might be military or sporting or dare-devil and the value is increased nearly twofold if the doll comes with its original box. The first British Action Man was Action Soldier, produced in 1966 under the name Palitoy, by Cascelloid of Leicester. The trade name was in honour of the firm's founder Mr A.E. Pallet who began making fancy rattles and small toys in 1919. Action Man is marked in relief on the back "Made in England by Palitoy under licence from Hasbro" with the copyright date 1964. Action Man's body is light flesh-coloured and he has a scar on one cheek. He is 11 in (28 cm) tall. Earlier dolls are better quality with static hands and painted hair. In the 1970s, real-looking hair was introduced and also gripping hands, followed by frowning 'eagle-like' eyes which moved, operated by a gadget on the back of the head. Among all of the 1980s Action Men pictured here, the Footballer is decidely the most popular, followed by the Red Devil and Superman and, lastly, the soldier doll. £30–40

▶ **BIONIC WOMAN**
Bionic Woman was
the brainchild of the
company Dennys
Fisher. She was a
spin-off from the
television programme
Bionic Man. She had
supposedly been
reconstructed after an
accident and had a
robot body beneath the
skin which gave her
superhuman powers.
Her excessively long
hair and 21st-century
look sets her apart
from other vinyl dolls.
£15–20
(boxed)

BEWARE
Inferior copies
are being made
in the Far East.
They are easily
identified as
they are usually
stamped "Made
in Taiwan" or
"Made in Japan".

◀ **SASHA DOLLS**
Sasha dolls were
designed by Sasha
Morgenthaler who was
born in Bern in 1893
and went to art school
thanks to the financial
assistance of artist
Paul Klee. She became
a sculptor before
marrying painter Ernst
Morgenthaler. In
the 1930s, she began
making dolls for her
three children and
was involved in
rescuing Jewish refugee
children from
Germany in 1940.
Her dream was to
create internationally
acceptable dolls,
not just dolls with
conventional pretty
features. Her high-
quality range which
has faces full of a
wistful innocence
has proved to be an
enormous hit with
children. In Britain,
Trendon Toys began
producing them in
1965. They were also
made in Germany
and America for
those markets.
£50–100 each

PART 6

INFORMATION

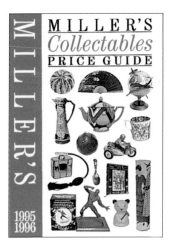

ABOVE A VALUABLE SOURCE ON PRICES.

LEFT SOTHEBY'S AUCTION CATALOGUE COVER.

WHERE TO SEE

Visiting major collections in museums and houses open to the public is a valuable way of learning about dolls and bears. Listed below are just some of the most noteworthy places. Costume collections are also worth exploring, since a knowledge of the history of fashion is helpful in knowing the dates of dolls.

GREAT BRITAIN

Bethnal Green Museum of Childhood
Cambridge Heath Road
London E2 9PA

London Toy and Model Museum
21–3 Craven Hill
London W2 3EN

The Teddy Bear Museum
19 Greenhill Street
Stratford-upon-Avon
Warwickshire CV37 6LF

Museum of Childhood
42 High St
Edinburgh
Lothian EH1 1TG

TEDDY BEAR & DOLL HOSPITALS
Teddy Bears
Sue Pearson
13 Prince Albert Street
The Lanes
Brighton
East Sussex BN1 1HE

Dolls
Yesterday's Child
Angel Arcade
118 Islington High Street
London N1 8EQ
(Wednesday & Saturday only)

WHERE TO BUY

Doll and teddy-bear fairs are held regularly around Britain and elsewhere. These are good places to learn as well as to buy. Look out for local advertisements.

GREAT BRITAIN
MAJOR AUCTION HOUSES
HOLDING SPECIAL SALES
Bonhams Chelsea
65–9 Lots Road
London SW10 0RN

Christie's South Kensington
85 Old Brompton Road
London SW7 3LD

Phillips Bayswater
10 Salem Road
London W2 4DI

Sotheby's
34–5 New Bond Street
London W1A 2AA

Sotheby's Sussex
Summers Place
Billingshurst
West Sussex RH14 9AD

SOME OF THE MANY SHOPS
Teddy Bears of Witney
99 High Street
Witney
Oxfordshire OX8 6LY
(Shop with museum display)

Sue Pearson
Antique Dolls & Teddy Bears
13 Prince Albert St
The Lanes
Brighton, East Sussex BN1 1HE

GLOSSARY

All-bisque Rare, mid-19th century German doll made exclusively from bisque.

Applied ears Ears applied to pressed doll's head; not integral.

Bald head Bisque head with a solid crown.

Bébé French term for doll's body with a short, chubby build, representing infant.

Beeswax A commercially useful wax secreted by worker bees and used in making dolls' heads in the late 18th century.

Bent-limb The term describing a covered, five-piece jointed body.

Biedermeier Style of furniture popular in Germany 1810–1840s; doll's-house furniture and papier-mâché, shoulder-headed doll.

Bisque or **biscuit** Malleable ceramic material with an unglazed surface used in making dolls' heads. Bisque can be poured into shape before being fired at a high temperature.

Bonnet head Doll wearing hat or bonnet moulded as an integral part of the head.

Boot-button eyes Black wooden eyes with metal loops on back, used in early teddy bears.

Breveté The French word for 'patented'. stamped on dolls as evidence of patent or registration; often abbreviated to *B.T.E.* or *Bte.*

Bust head American term for shoulder-head.

Burlap Term interchangeable in Europe for hessian. Course cloth made with single jute yarns. Used in making early bears.

Carton Material made from cardboard and composition, used for making dolls' bodies.

Celluloid Original trade name for pyroxylin, an early and highly flammable form of plastic used for making dolls; invented in the United States in 1869 by the Hyatt Bros.

Character doll A 20th-century doll with a realistic rather than idealized expression.

China Glazed porcelain used in making dolls' heads; popular in the mid-19th century.

Cloth doll The term for a doll made from fabric; sometimes known as a rag doll.

Composition Inexpensive substance made from cloth, size, wood, wood-pulp, plaster of Paris, glue and sawdust; used for dolls.

Crazing Tiny network of cracks which appear over time on surface of a doll's face, particularly on composition and wax dolls.

Dep An abbreviation of the French *deposé* or the German *Deponirt* indicating a registered patent; on French and German dolls.

Disc joint A joint made of discs of cardboard held in place by a metal pin; used to articulate soft toys and teddy bears.

Dolls' hospital Repair shop for the restoration of dolls; some also cater for teddy bears.

D.R.M.R. (*Deutsches Reichsgebrauchsmunster*) German term for the official governmental roll of registered patents.

Dutch A term for German (not Dutch) wooden dolls; word often found on heads of German wooden dolls.

Egg head A rare type of miniature doll moulded as a porcelain head only, no torso.

Elastic stringing Limbs of jointed dolls held together with elastic through the body.

Excelsior Soft mixture of long, thin wood-shavings; stuffing used for teddy bears.

Fashion doll A French lady doll, usually with a kid body and bisque head, dressed in elaborate and fashionable attire.

Fauteuil A French armchair, miniature examples made for 19th-century doll's houses.

Fixed eyes The term for simple glass eyes not moving; used on dolls and teddy bears.

Flange neck Type of head with ridge at base of neck, used mainly on soft-bodied dolls.

Flirty eyes Glass dolls' eyes that open, close and move from side to side.

Floating joint Limbs connected by sliding them over a loose or 'floating' ball.

Fontange A tall head-dress worn in the 17th and 18th centuries.

Four-headed doll Set produced by Kestner comprising a doll with a socket body and detachable head with interchangeable heads.

French joint Doll limbs attached to each other by a ball fixed to one of the limbs.

Frog's legs Flat, splayed legs found on soft-bodied German baby dolls, particularly those made by Armand Marseille.

Ges Shortening of *Gesch*, the German word for registration mark or patent.

Gesland Doll's body made from articulated wood or metal, padded with kapok, covered in stockinette; also doll repair company.

Gesso Plaster of Paris used as a base for painting on 18th-century wooden dolls.

Googly eyes Large, round eyes that glance to the side, originally found on dolls designed by Grace Grebbie Drayton.

Grödnertal Traditional wood-carving area in Germany famous for wooden dolls; slender-bodied, jointed doll popular throughout Germany in early-19th century.

Growler Voice box device inside a teddy bear that produces a growl or roar.

Gusseted Cloth or kid doll's body with insets to allow movement at the joints.

Gutta-percha Fibrous material used for dolls' bodies and heads, late-19th century.

Half-doll or **pin-cushion doll** Type of miniature doll popular from the early-20th century, for mounting on a pincushion or other accessory from a lady's boudoir.

Impressed Maker's mark is indented into surface of doll's head or shoulder-plate.

Incised Maker's mark is scratched into the surface of a doll's head or shoulder-plate.

Inserted hair Hair, either real or artificial, set into the scalp of wax dolls.

Intaglio eyes Painted eyes with concave pupils and irises, carved into a bisque head.

Jersey Originally made of wool on the island of Jersey but now of various fibres. Used for bears. Has no distinct rib.

Kapok Lightweight fibre from the tropical kapok tree; used for stuffing English and German teddy bears.

Kid Soft leather used for doll's bodies, generally with bisque heads, late-19th century.

Lowbrow Late-19th century, china-headed doll with short, curly hair low on forehead.

Marriage Doll constructed using limbs and a head that did not originally belong together.

Milliner's model Type of papier-mâché shoulder-headed doll with an elaborate hairstyle, popular during the 19th century.

Mitten hands/feet Dolls' hands or feet in block, no separate fingers and toes.

Mohair Long, white lustrous and dirt-resistant hair from the Angora goat native to Asia Minor. Generally used for dolls' hair and bears.

Moulded ears Ears cast as an intrinsic part of the head mould of a doll.

Moulded hair Hair that forms an intrinsic part of a doll's head.

Mould no. The recorded number of the mould used in producing a bisque-headed doll, impressed on head.

Muzzled bear Teddy bear wearing muzzle, introduced by Steiff in 1908. They were based on performing bears.

***Ne plus ultra* body** A body with *ne plus ultra* joints – i.e. jointed at knee and body – with a bisque shoulder-head. The body also forms part of the thigh. Introduced in 1883.

Nettle fibre Material resembling linen used by Steiff when materials were scarce during the First World War.

Open-closed mouth Doll's mouth appearing to be open but no opening between lips.

Open head Open-crowned head covered with a pate (either cork or cardboard) with wig attached. Found on most bisque dolls.

Painted bisque Bisque covered with a layer of paint but not fired, susceptible to flaking.

Paperweight eyes Realistic, blown-glass eyes with white threads running through the irises giving impression of depth; also known as spiral glass eyes. Often found on French bébés, particularly those that were produced by Jumeau.

Papier-mâché Combination of moulded paper pulp, whitening agent and glue, used during the 19th century for the construction of dolls' heads, bodies and furniture.

Parian Originally, a marble from Paros, Greece. In this sense, pure, untinted bisque made in imitation of real Parian; sometimes used on shoulder-headed dolls. Parian dolls generally have painted features and glass eyes.

Parisienne The term used by Jumeau to describe its fashion doll.

Pate A crown piece found under the wig that covers the hole in some dolls' heads; made from cardboard, cork or plaster.

Pedlar doll An early form of Grödnertal wooden doll, some dating back to the 1830s, which originally carried a tray or basket of wares in imitation of contemporary peddlars.

Peg doll or **peg wooden** An early wooden doll with simple, peg joints.

Penny wooden Inexpensive, wooden dolls of the late-19th century.

Piano baby All-bisque figurines of babies by Gebrüder Heubach, for display on piano.

Plush Warp pile fabric with a long, loosely woven cut pile. Used to imitate fur.

Polyurethane fibre Synthetic fabric, developed in Germany during the Second World War. Used for bear's fur.

Porcelain A fine glazed china used for making dolls' heads and limbs.

Portrait doll A term for early Jumeau and other dolls representing a particular person.

Poured wax Hollow head or shoulder-head made by repeated dipping into molten wax until a substantial shell results, then painted.

Pressed wax or **solid wax** Dolls with solid carved wax heads, made before poured wax.

Printed doll Features and details of a doll printed on fabric for home assembly,

Provenance The documented history of any antique item, including a doll, doll's house, teddy bear or furniture. May enhance value.

Pumpkin head A type of wax-over doll's head with moulded hair; popular in England and Germany in the mid-19th century.

Reproduction Any copy of an antique, including dolls made in moulds taken from an original doll or doll's head.

Rod bear An early type of Steiff teddy bear with metal rod jointing.

Sand baby Collectors' term for dolls produced by Käthe Kruse with heavy heads loosely attached to bodies filled with sand.

S.F.B.J. Initials of the *Société Française de Fabrication des Bébés et Jouets*, association of French dollmakers that was formed at the end of the 19th century.

S.G.D.G. (*Sans Garantie du Gouvernement*) meaning 'without government guarantee'; an unregistered trademark on French dolls.

S.I.C. (*Société industrielle de Celluloid*) French organization, initials on some celluloid dolls.

Shadow box Glass-fronted box constructed as a decorative setting and intended for the display of wax-over and early slit-head dolls.

Shoulder-head The term for a doll's head and shoulders moulded in one piece.

Shoulder-plate Area of a doll's shoulder-head below the neck.

Sleep eyes Glass doll's eyes open when doll is upright and close when laid horizontally.

Slit head A wax-over-papier-mâché doll made in England in the early-19th century.

Solid-domed head Socket or shoulder-plate bisque doll's head with crown made from bisque; also known as **Belton heads**.

Solid wax see **Pressed wax**

Socket head Type of swivel head with a rounded base to neck, enabling head to fit into top of body. Most common head.

Spade hands Crude hands with little detail, found on early German wooden dolls.

Stockinette A fabric used on the bodies of fashion dolls made by Gesland and others.

Stump doll Doll in single piece of wood.

Swivel head Doll's head made separately from shoulder-plate, allows head to swivel.

Talking doll A doll with mechanism which can give the impression of 'talking'.

Tenon joint A type of joint used on the bodies of wooden fashion dolls.

Two-faced doll Rare doll with revolving head turning to reveal either of two faces; operated by hidden knob in top of head.

Vinyl A non-flammable, flexible yet tough form of plastic that was used for dolls from the 1940s, and which virtually replacing hard plastic by the 1950s.

Voice box The internal mechanical device which enables a doll to 'cry' or 'sing'.

Watermelon mouth A thin-lipped, smiling mouth found on googly-eyed dolls.

Wax-over-composition A head or shoulder-head made of composition covered with wax; often shortened to 'wax-over'.

Wig pull The small flakes of bisque accidentally removed by pulling off a wig.

Wire eyes Eyes closing by wire connection.

Wire springing Heads of Jumeau dolls are attached to their bodies with a wire spring.

Yorkshire cloth Cloth often used by Farnell in making teddy bears, alternative to mohair plush. Also used by other manufacturers.

WHAT TO READ

GENERAL

Cieslik, Jurgen and Marianne,
    The German Encyclopedia of Dolls, 1985
Coleman, Elizabeth Anne, Dorothy and
    Evelyn Jane,
    The Collector's Encyclopedia of Dolls –
    Volume I 1968;
    Volume II 1986
Darbyshire, Lydia, *The Collector's*
    Encyclopedia of Toys and Dolls, 1990
Ernshaw, Nora, *Collector's Dolls,* 1987
Foulke, Jan, *Blue Book of*
    Dolls and Values 1991,
    Doll Classics 1987
Gibbs, Tyson, *The Collector's*
    Encyclopedia of Black Dolls, 1987
Goodfellow, Caroline G.,
    Understanding Dolls, 1983
King, Constance Eileen,
    The Collector's History of Dolls, 1977
Mandeville, A. Glenn, *Doll Fashion Anthology,*
    1987
Pollock, *Pollock's Dictionary of*
    English Dolls, 1982
Richter, Lydia, *Baby Dolls,* 1989
Taylor, Kerry, *The Letts Guide to*
    Collecting Dolls, 1990
Theriault, Florence,
    Dolls – The Early Years
    1780–1889, 1989
White, Gwen, *European and*
    American Dolls, 1966

WAX DOLLS

Hillier, Mary, *The History of*
    Wax Dolls, 1985

FASHION DOLLS

Earnshaw, Nora, *Collecting Dolls,* 1996
King, Constance Eileen, *Jumeau,*
    King of Dollmakers, 1983
Tarnowska, Marie, *Fashion Dolls,* 1986
Theimer, François, *The Bru Book,* 1991

BÉBÉS

McGonagle, Dorothy A.,
    The Dolls of Jules Nicholas Steiner, 1988

CHARACTER DOLLS

Axe, John, *Kewpie Dolls and Art,* 1987
Cieslik, Jurgen and Marianne, *German Doll*
    Marks and Identification Book, 1986
Foulke, Jan, *Kestner, King of Dollmakers,* 1982;
    Simon & Halbig – The Artful Aspect, 1984
Tarnowska, Marie, *Rare Character Dolls,* 1987

FABRIC & RAG DOLLS

Cieslik, Jurgen and Marianne,
    Button In The Ear, 1989
Judd, Polly, *Cloth Dolls of the*
    1920s and '30s – Identification
    and Price Guide, 1990
Richter, Lydia, *Treasury of*
    Käthe Kruse Dolls, 1984

COMPOSITION, CELLULOID & PLASTIC

De Wein, *The Collector's Encyclopedia of*
    Barbie Dolls, 1977
Judd, Polly and Pamela, *Hard Plastic*
    Doll Identification and
    Price Guide, 1985
Buchholz, Shirley, *A Century of*
    Celluloid Dolls, 1983

TEDDY BEARS

Axe, John, *The Magic of Merrythought,* 1986
Brewster, Kim and Rossel Waugh, Carol-Lyn
    The Official Price Guide to
    Antique and Modern Teddy Bears, 1988
Cockrill, Pauline,
    The Teddy Bear Encyclopedia, 1995
Hillier, Mary, *The Teddy Bear –*
    A Celebration, 1985
Mullins, Linda, *Teddy Bears Past & Present,*
    A Collector's Identification Guide, 1986
Pearson, Sue, *Bears,* 1995
Pistorius, Rolfs Christel, *Steiff Sensational*
    Teddy Bears, Animals & Dolls, 1991
Schoonmaker, Patricia,
    The Collector's History of
    the Teddy Bear, 1981
Sieventing, Helen,
    Teddy Bear & Friends Price Guide, 1988
Stratton, Deborah, *Bearland,* 1992

INDEX

ACKNOWLEDGMENTS

The publishers would like to thank the following people and companies for supplying pictures for use in this book or for allowing their pieces to be photographed:

Back jacket Tim Ridley at Sotheby's for Reed; **back flap** Sotheby's; **front jacket tl**Reed, **tc**Sotheby's, **tr**Tim Ridley at Farnham Antiques Centre for Reed, **bl**Sotheby's, **br**Sotheby's; **front flap** Sotheby's; 2 Sotheby's (x8); **3tl, tr** and **br**Sotheby's, **bl** Tim Ridley at Farnham Antiques Centre for Reed, **bc**Tim Ridley at Sotheby's for Reed; 10 Tim Ridley at Sotheby's for Reed; 11 Tim Ridley at Sotheby's for Reed; 12 Tim Ridley at Sotheby's for Reed; **13tl**Sotheby's, **br**Tim Ridley at Farnham Antiques Centre for Reed; 14 © Christie's/photograph by Michael Pritchard; 15 Sotheby's; 16 Sotheby's; 17 Tim Ridley at Sotheby's for Reed; 18 Ian Pout; 19 Ian Pout; 20 Tim Ridley at Farnham Antiques Centre for Reed; **21tl**Reed/ckl, **br**Christie's South Kensington; 22 Sotheby's; 23 Tim Ridley at Sotheby's for Reed; 24 Tim Ridley at Sotheby's for Reed; 25 Sotheby's; 26 Sotheby's; 27 Sotheby's; **28tl** and **br**Sotheby's; 29 **tl** and **br**Sotheby's; **30bl**Reed/ckl (x2), **tr**Sotheby's; **31**Sotheby's; **32**Sotheby's; **33**Sotheby's; **34l**Robin Saker at Sotheby's Sussex for Reed, **b** and **r**Sotheby's; **35l**Sotheby's, **c**Reed/ckl (x2), **r**Tim Ridley at Farnham Antiques Centre for Reed (x2); **39br**Tim Ridley at Farnham Antiques Centre for Reed; **42l**Reed/ckl, **c** and **l**Reed/Sue Pearson; **43l**Reed/ckl, **c**Sotheby's, **bl**Tim Ridley at Farnham Antiques Centre for Reed, **r**Reed/ckl; **44**Sue Pearson (x2); **45cl**Reed/Sue Pearson, **bl**Christie's South Kensington, **c** and **bc**Reed/Isabelle Eddington, **r**Sotheby's; 46 Sotheby's; **47**Reed/Sue Pearson; **48**Sotheby's; **49bl**Sotheby's, **c**Reed, **tr**Robin Saker at Sotheby's Sussex for Reed, **br**Tim Ridley at Farnham Antiques Centre for Reed; **50bl**Sotheby's, **c and t**Robin Saker at Ian Pout for Reed; **51bl**Sotheby's, **c**Robin Saker at Ian Pout for Reed (x3), **r**Sotheby's; **52t**Reed/Sue Pearson, **b**Robin Saker at Ian Pout for Reed; 53 Robin Saker at Ian Pout for Reed (x2); 54 Robin Saker at Ian Pout for Reed (x2); **55tl, tr** and **br**Robin Saker at Ian Pout for Reed, **bl** and **c**Reed/Dottie Ayers; **56**Sotheby's; **57tl**Sotheby's, **br**Christie's South Kensington, **bl**Tim Ridley at Farnham Antiques Centre for Reed, **c**Robin Saker at Ian Pout for Reed; **58bl**Robin Saker at Ian Pout for Reed, **c**Sotheby's, **br**Reed; **59l** and **b**Robin Saker at Ian Pout for Reed, **tr**R; **60t**Robin Saker at Sotheby's Sussex for Reed, **c**Reed/Sue Pearson, **b**Robin Saker at Sotheby's Sussex; **61 l** and **c**Reed/Sue Pearson, **br**Tim Ridley at Farnham Antiques Centre for Reed; **62l**Reed/Dottie Ayers, **r**Sotheby's; **63l and t**Robin Saker at Ian Pout for Reed, **tr** and **br**Reed; **64**Tim Ridley at Farnham Antiques Centre for Reed; **65tl**Tim Ridley at Farnham Antiques Centre for Reed, **c**Robin Saker at Ian Pout for Reed, **r**Ian Booth at Sue Pearson for Reed; **66l** and **tr**Reed/Sue Pearson, **br**Tim Ridley at Farnham Antiques Centre for Reed; **67t**Tim Ridley at Farnham Antiques Centre for Reed, **cl** and **bl**Reed/Sue Pearson, **br**Robin Saker at Sotheby's Sussex for Reed; **68l**Robin Saker at Ian Pout for Reed, **r**Tim Ridley at Farnham Antiques Centre for Reed, **b**Sue Pearson; **69t**Robin Saker at Ian Pout for Reed, **bl and r**Tim Ridley at Farnham Antiques Centre for Reed; **70t**©Disney/Tim Ridley at Farnham Antiques Centre for Reed, **bl** and **br**©Beaverbrook Newspapers/Tim Ridley at Farnham Antiques Centre for Reed; **71bl**Robin Saker at Ian Pout for Miller's, **r**Tim Ridley at Farnham Antiques Centre for Reed; 72 Sotheby's; **73t**Sotheby's, **r**Ian Booth at Sue Pearson for Miller's, **b**Bunny Campione (x3); **74t**Sotheby's, **c** and **r**Ian Booth at Sue Pearson for Miller's; **75tr**Sue Pearson, **c**Miller's at Lorraine Tarrant Antiques, **br**Sue Pearson; **76t**Sotheby's, **b**Tim Ridley at Farnham Antiques Centre for Reed; **77**Tim Ridley at Farnham Antiques Centre for Reed (x2); **78tl**Sotheby's, **r**Tim Ridley at Farnham Antiques Centre for Reed, **b**©Disney/Tim Ridley at Farnham Antiques Centre for Reed; **79t**Tim Ridley at Farnham Antiques Centre for Reed, **l** and **b**Ian Booth at Sue Pearson for Miller's; **80t**Robin Saker at Ian Pout for Reed, **b**Tim Ridley at Farnham Antiques Centre for Reed; **81t**Robin Saker at Farnham Antiques Centre for Reed, **c**Ian Booth at Sue Pearson for Miller's, **b**Miller's at The Magpie's Nest; 82 Sotheby's; 83 Sotheby's; 84 Sotheby's; 85 Sotheby's; 86 Sotheby's (x3), 87 Sotheby's (x3); 88 Sotheby's (x4); 89 Sotheby's (x2); 90 Sotheby's (x3); 91 Sotheby's (x4); 92 Sotheby's (x3); 93 Sotheby's (x2); 94 Sotheby's (x3); 95 Sotheby's (x3); 96 Sotheby's; 97 Sotheby's (x2); 98 Robin Saker at Sotheby's Sussex for Reed; **99t**Sotheby's, **c**Christie's South Kensington, **br**Reed/Sue Pearson; 100 Sotheby's (x2); **101tl** and **c**Sotheby's, **b**Reed/Jackie Allington; **102l**Christie's South Kensington, **r**Robin Saker at Sotheby's Sussex for Reed;

103 Sotheby's (x3); 104lReed/Sue Pearson and rChristies's South Kensington; 105tl, tc and rRobin Saker at Sotheby's Sussex for Reed, bChristie's South Kensington; 106c and rSotheby's; 107Robin Saker at Sotheby's Sussex for Reed (x3); 108tl and trRobin Saker at Sotheby's Sussex for Reed, blReed/Sue Pearson, brSotheby's; 109Robin Saker at Sotheby's Sussex for Reed (x3);110Sotheby's; 111tlSotheby's (x4); 112lChristie's South Kensington, rSotheby's, bSotheby's; 113c and blSotheby's; 114 Sotheby's (x2); 115 Sotheby's (x2); 116 Sotheby's (x2); 117 Sotheby's (x4); 118 Sotheby's (x2); 119 Sotheby's (x3); 120 Sotheby's (x2); 121tlReed/Sue Pearson, blChristie's South Kensington, trChristie's South Kensington, brSotheby's; 122 Sotheby's (x2); 123 Sotheby's (x3); 124 Sotheby's (x3);125tReed/Pam Walker, r and bSotheby's; 126lReed/Pam Walker, rSotheby's; 127tlReed/Sue Pearson, brSotheby's (x2);128Sotheby's, 129trSotheby's (x2); 130blSotheby's, trReed/Sue Pearson; 131tr and blSotheby's, brReed/Sue Pearson; 132 Christie's South Kensington (x4); 133blChristie's South Kensington, rSotheby's; 134tSotheby's, lReed/Sue Pearson, rChristie's South Kensington; 135 Robin Saker at Sotheby's Sussex for Reed (x5); 136 Sotheby's (x2); 137tl, tr and brSotheby's, cl and blReed/Pat Walker; 138 Miller's at Farnham Antiques Centre; 139lSotheby's, tr, cr and brRobin Saker at Sotheby's Sussex for Reed; 140 Sotheby's; 141cChristie's South Kensington, blSotheby's; 142 Robin Saker at Sotheby's Sussex for Reed (x3); 143blSotheby's, cRobin Saker at Sotheby's Sussex for Reed; 144blTim Ridley at Farnham Antiques Centre for Reed, rReed/Pam Walker; 145tRobin Saker at Sotheby's Sussex for Reed (x2), brReed/Sue Pearson; 146tl and bRobin Saker at Sotheby's Sussex for Reed, trSotheby's; 147trReed/Sue Pearson, clSotheby's, bReed/Sue Pearson; 148cSotheby's (x4); 149tSotheby's (x4), bReed/Dottie Ayers; 150lTim Ridley at Farnham Antiques Centre for Reed, rChristie's South Kensington, bReed/Sue Pearson; 151trReed/Sue Pearson, bRobin Saker at Sotheby's Sussex for Reed; 152 lReed/Dottie Ayers, cReed/Dottie Ayers, rReed/Sue Pearson; 153l and cChristie's South Kensington, rTim Ridley at Farnham Antiques Centre for Reed; 154trReed/Dottie Ayers, cReed/Sue Pearson, brBunny Campione; 155tc and tr Bunny Campione, cl and blSotheby's; 156c and blRobin Saker at Sotheby's Sussex for Reed; 157Tim Ridley at Farnham Antiques Centre for Reed (x4); 158Tim Ridley at Farnham Antiques Centre (x3); 159Tim Ridley at Farnham Antiques Centre (x2); 160Tim Ridley at Farnham Antiques Centre (x3); 161 Tim Ridley at Farnham Antiques Centre for Reed (x), brChristie's South Kensington; 162 Miller's; 163tMiller's at Frances Baird, b Miller's; 164 Sotheby's; 165 Reed

Key
t top, c centre, b bottom, l left, r right
EGR Frances Baird, The Anchorage, Wrotham Road, Culverstone, Meopham, Kent
Lorraine Tarrant Antiques, 7–11 Market Place, Ringwood, Hampshire
The Magpie's Nest, 14 Palace Street, Canterbury, Kent

Special photography by Tim Ridley, Ian Booth and Robin Saker for Reed Books and Miller's.

Illustrations on pp. 37–7, 38–9, 40–1, 110, 113, 140, 143, 148, 135 by Simon Miller

Author Acknowledgments
With special thanks to:
Gisela Barrington, Sue Pearson, Ian Pout, Marilyn Russ, Maureen Stanford.